## ADVANCE PRAISE

*"Allen Giese has written a book that everyone needs when parenting a child or young adult with a serious mental illness—or any serious health condition. It offers otherwise hard-to-find practical advice and step-by-step thinking about managing a family's finances when chronic conditions emerge and worsen."*

—PAUL GIONFRIDDO, PRESIDENT AND
CEO, MENTAL HEALTH AMERICA

*"Long overdue, this book addresses the financial impact that mental illness places on the family and offers helpful advice and steps you can take to be proactive about your family's future financial security."*

—MARY GILIBERTI, CEO, NATIONAL
ALLIANCE ON MENTAL ILLNESS

*"Combining his personal experience as a parent of a special-needs child and years as a financial planner, Allen Giese has written a comprehensive guide on what you need to know to navigate the financial impact of a child's mental illness and the steps a family can take to be proactive about their financial future."*

—DAVE BUTLER, CO-CEO AND HEAD OF
GLOBAL FINANCIAL ADVISOR SERVICES,
DIMENSIONAL FUND ADVISORS

*"Who is going to take care of my kid when I'm gone? That's what every parent of a special-needs child wants to know. Allen Giese helps you answer that question with this book."*

—EDNA EINHORN, PRESIDENT, NAMI-BROWARD

*"Finally, there's a guide for those families with financial means, but with concerns about an adult child managing those finances, in a way that lays out a plan so the money is there for their benefit for years to come."*

—PAUL F. JAQUITH, LCSW, CAP, PRESIDENT/CEO,
MENTAL HEALTH ASSOCIATION OF SOUTHEAST FLORIDA

# WHEN MENTAL ILLNESS STRIKES

# WHEN
# MENTAL ILLNESS
# STRIKES

## Crisis Intervention for
## the Financial Plan

## ALLEN GIESE

## LIONCREST
PUBLISHING

WHEN MENTAL ILLNESS STRIKES

*Crisis Intervention for the Financial Plan*

ISBN   978-1-5445-1108-5  *Hardcover*

978-1-5445-1107-8  *Paperback*

978-1-5445-1106-1  *Ebook*

*To Gayle, my love, my wife and partner in life, who has supported me in this and every project. And to Andrew, whose courage measures beyond anyone's I know.*

# Contents

# Introduction

You think you're on a path in life...until everything changes.

Life changed completely for my wife and me the night friends invited us to a Yom Kippur dinner. My son was seventeen at the time, was in his last year in high school, and had been getting increasingly anxious for months. That night, as we made the half-hour drive to our friends' house, he was clearly becoming more uncomfortable. At the dinner, he couldn't sit still. He kept going outside. His anxiety got so severe that we finally made the decision to leave.

By the time we got back to the house, my son had taken a big step away from reality. He was pacing frenetically around our pool. He clutched his hands together and contorted his fingers under his chin, like he had in high-stress situations since he was a kid, his fingers going white from the tension. He seemed terrified of everything around him. We didn't understand what was happening. We were dumbfounded and scared, wanting to help but not knowing how.

In retrospect, his illness had been building for months, even years, before that break. He'd been a high achiever in school, the top player on his school tennis team. He'd excelled in geography and math and was becoming a good guitar player. But the last year or so he was having a progressively more difficult time with his school work. His anxiety was building to the point it was taking over his life, and he was getting painfully shy. He began distancing himself from old friends, and he'd found some new friends we didn't like. We found out later he had been smoking pot with them regularly. I believe he was trying to self-medicate away his anxiety, but for people with a genetic propensity for mental illness, some studies have indicated marijuana use may bring on symptoms earlier and with more severity. In retrospect, it may have been one of the worst things he could have done.

My son graduated high school, barely, finishing up his coursework online amid the whirl of doctor's visits and treatments and psychosis, but his grip on reality stayed loose. We began our search in earnest for something that would cure him. We spent large amounts of time and money chasing treatment after treatment, only to see him sinking deeper into the grip of the disease taking hold of his brain. Eventually, my son was diagnosed with schizophrenia. He is now twenty-seven, and while we have all gained a much better understanding of what has happened to him, he is still battling the disease that has changed all of our lives.

For my son and our entire family, that day changed everything.

## A TRADITIONAL PATH INTERRUPTED

My family had been on a traditional path: two kids, a house, and a growing business. With my oldest in high school, I was worried about funding their college, growing my new business, and retiring one day. Mental illness was not on my radar.

Both kids had been doing well. My son and daughter were very involved in school, had a lot of friends, and my son was excelling in both school and athletics. Back in Little League, his coach would put him on the mound in high-pressure situations, when the bases were loaded and it was the bottom of an inning. My son would go in, throw the strikes that were needed, and get the kid out. But he'd do an odd thing with his fingers between pitches, contorting them together close to his chest below his chin—an incredible amount of tension turning his knuckles white. He'd turn his chin downward, and you could see the stress in his face. It seemed to be his way of releasing huge amounts of tension and staying focused on the moment.

As a sophomore in high school, he had the opportunity to transfer into an accelerated gifted program. We all agreed it was a good opportunity, since his grades had always been good and we had high hopes for his college. In retrospect, the transfer put a lot more pressure on him. After he started the new program, the anxiety and shyness escalated, and he started losing the friends he'd been so close to just a few years before. Things built and built until the break.

We had some warning, though I didn't listen. His mentor through church, a close friend of ours and a first responder for years, told me after a short trip that he'd been afraid my son was going to jump out of the car on the highway while they were driving. He said, "Listen, I don't know how to tell you this, but you may be dealing with something very serious here."

I laughed him off at the time. Honestly, I'd been in the car with my friend, and his driving nearly made me want to jump out too!

## SIGNS OF THE STRUGGLE

The finger contortions my son had made when he'd been on the pitcher's mound at Little League had always been a part of everyday life. The gesture is cartoonish, like an evil persona crouching over, rubbing his hands together. Only, unlike the cartoons, he makes no sound. His fingers get curled and tight, tightening up with so much tension they shake a little. He'd done this since he was a kid, under stress or when he was studying or trying to focus. After his first psychotic break at seventeen, the gesture became prolonged, and his whole body would get tense, wound up like a ball of string. We've since learned that this kind of gesture can often be an early indicator of schizophrenia. These days, we know if we see the hands tightening, it's a sign he's on the precipice of anxiety and crisis.

My son, who always seemed easygoing, is socially awkward and shy now. As the shyness—and his illness—was setting in, I talked to him about taking steps to make friends, but his problem went deeper than that. He had trouble talking to people, especially peers. Authority figures like teachers were easier, but even those are hard now. My formerly health-obsessed kid now smokes up to two packs a day.

One event vividly illustrates the progression of my son's condition: he went to an event at our church for teens, and he called me out of the blue, his voice frantic. He begged me to come pick him up. We knew by then he was coping with extreme anxiety. I went, planning to give him some kind of fatherly words of wisdom, asking him to go back and face his fear. When I got there, however, he ran out of the building, jumped in the car, and said, "We have to go, now, now, now!" It was like a scene from an action movie. The anxiety was so severe, I left with him—calling the event coordinator on my cell phone so she knew he was gone. It was the only way he would calm down. I worried there was something deeply wrong.

## A LONG PATH TO DIAGNOSIS

We tried to help my son with his worsening anxiety. Traditional psychotherapy didn't seem to help, and we got increasingly bewildered and frustrated. I initially trusted the psychotherapy professionals, since I'm a professional in the field of finance. I thought that they, like I, understood what they were doing in their own field. As time went on, it became obvious that the psychologists we saw didn't understand at all. Perhaps this illness was just out of their league.

It took over a year to get him diagnosed with schizophrenia, which I've learned is typical. I cannot emphasize enough how hard it was during this process. We felt like we were wasting time and money and were no better off. No one seemed to understand what was going on with him; his disease hadn't manifested fully yet, and the specialists were only seeing his very best face at that point. Worse, we didn't have the background or experience to insist they do anything differently. We were completely dependent on the experts, and the experts had to rule out dozens of alternatives as the disease progressed before schizophrenia was even on their radar. You can't take a blood test to diagnose mental illness.

We first went to a psychologist for my son's anxiety when he was fifteen—but of course, it was more than anxiety. I remember in one appointment with a new psychologist he rapidly became more and more agitated to the point he was about to explode right there in the office; he stood up, frantic, and said he had to leave the room. The psychologist told him outside the back door there was a walking path along the lake, and he left to walk around that lake.

The psychologist turned to me and said, "Wow, did you see that?"

I was dumbfounded. Here, of all people, was the one person who was supposed to be *not* surprised about this, and he was shocked. My son was in serious pain, and he'd never seen it before. This happened over and over again. We went through "experts" like tissue paper, and nothing seemed to help.

My wife, Gayle, got referrals from other people, and we tried yet more experts. Meanwhile, she got more and more involved with NAMI, the National Alliance on Mental Illness, as well as other local groups she could find for support. Taking care of our son became her full-time job: doing research, taking him to doctor's appointments, and doing all the day-to-day things we had to take care of at that point. I don't know what we would have done if she hadn't already been retired from a full-time position and worked only a flexible, part-time job as a church musician. I was building a business at the time, and we relied on that for almost all our income. If that wasn't the case, she would have had to retire in order to help our son.

Finally, one psychologist we had recently seen called us on a Sunday afternoon. "I think I know what's going on with your son," he said. "I think he has a schizotypal disorder."

This was kind of like saying, "He has some symptoms of schizophrenia but we don't want to call it that yet." I had no idea what schizophrenia was—I thought schizophrenia was when someone had multiple personalities, which was totally wrong. It has nothing to do with multiple personalities; it has everything to do with him having massive anxiety, being disorganized, and having unusual thoughts and delusions. He, like many others with this illness, developed occasional hallucinations later.

Somehow having a word for what was wrong made it just a little easier to understand.

## THE FINANCE PIECE

I realized one day that the financial plan we'd been following for years was no longer adequate—and I was a financial planner! I hadn't even considered what we'd paid that the insurance didn't cover, what the dozens of psychologist and psychiatrist visits had cost, or the costs of his hospitalizations. He was my son. I was going to do everything in my power to help him.

I've since learned this total focus on my son's illness and how to help him is a typical approach. Gayle and I are very lucky in that, since I had a successful business with a good income, we could afford to pay for my son's treatments and tolerate a substantial amount of inefficiency and waste in the process. On the other side, I've since met parents who have gone through the same kind of spending on early treatments and who got into a high amount of debt over it, well over their heads.

In those first years, taking care of our son was all-consuming. We tried all the doctors we could possibly try. We flew to Vancouver to talk to a doctor who'd had success with diet and vitamin regimens. Unfortunately, the amount of vitamins he'd have to take was literally a large handful, three times a day. As soon as I understood that dairy could no longer be part of his diet, I knew it was doomed. Imagine telling an eighteen-year-old he can't have pizza! Nothing worked, but everything cost money, and little or nothing outside of traditional treatment was covered by insurance, even though we filed many claims with our health insurer, never getting a response. We bounced around among psychiatrists, medications, insurance plans—whatever it took to find the right dosage and combination to keep our son on an even keel. Until we got the meds right (or at least, close to right), we never knew what he was going to do. He'd keep us up night after night until we were nearly psychotic ourselves with lack of sleep. No matter how hard it got, though, Gayle and I were determined to stand by our son.

Even with all the resources we had, one day, I woke up to how incredibly costly the diagnosis and early treatment had been—not just the emotional toll, but the financial one, too. By then we had gotten the diagnosis of schizophrenia and ridden out those first few years of frantic hope. We began to understand the options we had for forcible hospitalization here in Florida for true emergencies, and we at least understood how life was going to be. We were still trying to find meds that worked and still trying to convince our son to take them, despite unpleasant side effects. We'd settled down into the acceptance that our son was unable to work. Although he may get much better, it's likely he will battle this illness for the rest of his life. This moment—the moment when you realize the illness is forever—is the point when some people throw in the towel and kids end up on the street—the most painful thing I could possibly imagine. Gayle and I were determined that no matter what happened, we would be there for our son, but our determination had consequences. Our son would need some level of care for his entire lifetime, not just the portion of it when Gayle and I were still living. We would have to find a way to provide for his daily needs after we were gone. I realized that, financially, I now had to make plans not only for Gayle's and my retirement, but for my son's expenses for his entire lifetime as well.

That realization meant I had to completely reconsider our plan, at my age, and start from scratch.

## A CRISIS TEAM FOR OUR FINANCES

It turns out that traditional approaches to situations involving severe mental illness can lead to bad outcomes, and that's as true of policing as it is of finances, as it happens. One of the gravest concerns many parents of mentally ill adult children have is that our children will be killed by police officers trained in only traditional methods. Law enforcement officers are often first responders to a person in crisis. Unfortunately, traditional policing often tends to escalate force in order to get control of a situation as quickly as possible. With a person having a mental health crisis, counter-aggressive behavior from the well-meaning police officer can be very ineffective and even harmful. If escalation continues, the police officer may feel threatened, and the person with mental illness may end up tased, shot, or in jail. It is my (and every parent's) nightmare that this will happen to my child.

Fortunately, the traditional training is not the only training out there. As part of our son's illness, we became aware of an amazing training program many municipalities offer—or sometimes require—their officers to take: Crisis Intervention Team training, or CIT. Officers go through forty hours of intensive classes and field visits learning how to deal with somebody who's in crisis from a mental illness. When we'd call 911 when my son was in crisis, we learned to specifically ask for an officer with this valuable and sometimes life-saving CIT training.

In contrast to a traditionally trained officer, the officer with this training is trained not to escalate the situation, instead allowing the person with mental illness time and space to stabilize. They'll let someone yell if it's not hurting anything, and they'll let someone approach the officer if it's not hurting anything. A CIT officer would talk calmly with my son, assuring him he's there to help him even if his behavior seemed "crazy." The officer would offer to take him somewhere where he could feel safe, which my son would often agree to peaceably. I cannot emphasize enough how important this training has been to us.

Traditional financial planning, like traditional policing, just doesn't do the job when it comes to family finances with severe mental illness involved. Most planners are trained on a transactional investment level. They sell financial products. In contrast, the right choices for families going through mental illness with adult children often don't involve financial products a broker or insurance agent can sell them. Instead, it's about financial counseling to avoid mistakes that could greatly cost your children as you pass on money to the next generation. It's about making wise, often non-common-sense choices that give your children the best possible future. For example, a traditional plan would have you make your child a beneficiary on your life insurance, but this will cost them their Medicare and Social Security income. So, instead, I counsel parents to consider alternatives, which we'll talk about later.

In the same way police officers handling severe mental illness in a traditional way can make things worse, handling this situation with traditional financial planning strategies can do the same. I wrote this book to address this problem and to share what I've learned in my life and through the lives of the other parents I've worked with. You need a specialty approach to this specialty situation.

If you're reading this book, you're likely through the desperate early years where you're just trying to figure out what's going on. You're ready to put some of your focus back on your finances. You're focused on ensuring you're making good decisions for your entire family for many years to come.

Financial planning can start as simply as saying no to the hyper-expensive treatments you truly can't afford. It's a sad truth that how effective treatments are in the world of mental health and how much they cost aren't related at all. We tried more than our fair share of expensive options, and they didn't help my son nearly as much as the state-funded program that he's in now.

Even once you've settled on treatment that's working, you'll want to look for options to pay for it all that don't mean wiping out your retirement account or going into heavy debt. Depending on your individual situation, those options may very well exist! I'll go through some of the options in the following chapters. Even if your resources are limited, however, knowing what you have, what your options are, and how to decide can take much of the weight of worry off your shoulders. It's easier to prioritize now, knowing the trade-offs, than to end up in a desperate situation down the road due to lack of planning.

Serious mental illness is one of the hardest things a family can go through; there's no need for the financial piece to be as distressing as it sometimes feels. This book is here to help. When you understand your options, you are empowered to make the best choices at the best times to help your family.

## WHY AM I GIVING BACK?

As a result of my experience with our son's mental illness, in the last few years, I've become more and more involved in the community of families dealing with similar issues. As a financial planner, I had a front-row seat to see how impactful severe mental illness is on the finances of families, and I found myself fielding question after question. Those questions, and the research I've done to understand them, along with the unique needs of families with mental illness in finance, ultimately led to this book. I want to give back to the community that has given me so much.

I first found the community in the Family-to-Family class I took from NAMI, the National Alliance on Mental Illness. Gayle had heard about the program and suggested I go, and I'm glad she did. In the class, for the first time, I truly understood what schizophrenia was. I learned it was a brain disease and not an emotional one, a disease like cancer but so much more stigmatized. That class was a watershed moment for me, as I realized what my son was going through and how important it was to give him good support. I also realized, looking around at the other parents in the room, that I wasn't the only one going through this. In fact, my experience wasn't even unusual. Schizophrenia affects 1.1 percent of the population or roughly 3.5 million people in the United States.

NAMI was started in my childhood hometown, Madison, Wisconsin, in 1979 by two moms determined to fight back against the stigma toward mental illness through education and awareness, and it's grown from there. In Florida, where I now live, there are more than twenty-five local chapters, each providing programs to help people understand more about mental illnesses like schizophrenia, bipolar disorder, anxiety, OCD, and depression.

I can tell you from my experience that knowledge changed everything. Knowing what the disease was, what all the confusing names of the meds were, and what research was being done to battle serious mental illness made it less mystical and gave me hope that one day we'll actually find a cure. Talking to other parents, seeing their children acting in so many of the same ways my son was, brought home to me that we aren't in this alone, and there are many others dealing with the same challenges.

I became highly involved with the local NAMI and Mental Health America (MHA) chapters. I realized how much discrimination and prejudice there was against mental illness in society, and I became determined to do my part to fight it. Only by talking about the problem can anyone get help for it, and only by talking about their own issues can the families of those with mental illness get the support they need. NAMI and MHA were deeply impactful on our lives, providing incredible support and free resources for me and my wife as we struggled to come to terms with our new reality.

A few years later in 2015, I wanted to ride my bike from San Diego, California, to St. Augustine, Florida, for charity. Gayle and I knew immediately that the charity had to somehow involve mental illness awareness. We founded Ride to Awareness and recruited ten cyclists to ride all or part of the trip with me, crossing the country promoting awareness and advocacy for mental illness.

As a result of the trip, we ended up raising nearly $100,000 in donations to support the ride. What we didn't use for our costs, we donated to NAMI and MHA chapters all along the path of the ride. I became a spokesman as I got interviewed for TV and articles. I studied to make sure I knew what I was talking about, and I ended up learning a lot about mental illness and the stigma keeping families quiet. I will never forget the conversations I had with families along that trip.

The Ride to Awareness team taking a break for a photo op. The South Florida MHA chapter asked us for a picture of us along our cross-country route, wearing these tie-dye T-shirts they made. I believe we took this picture somewhere in New Mexico. It was very hot!

During the ride, everywhere we went, people saw our thirty-four-foot RV covered in bright colors, emblazoned with information about mental health awareness. Everywhere we stopped, we'd open up the RV and people would start gathering around. They'd tell us the stories of their kid, their parent, their cousin, or their friend with mental illness and what that experience was like. The first day of the ride out of San Diego, two of our riders dropped off the back of the pack. A few minutes later, we realized they weren't there and stopped to wait. A half hour later, they came riding up; someone had pulled them over on the side of the road, desperate to talk about her brother who had battled mental illness and unfortunately just two weeks earlier had committed suicide.

People needed to tell their stories, but they had nowhere to tell them. The messages on the RV and our ride gear told them we were safe. They could talk to us. And they did, every day of the ride. Until that trip, I never really understood the depth and breadth of the issue of mental health in America. It is everywhere, in every social group, in every class, in every age. It affects everyone.

Once I got back, the stories continued—with a change. At a charity event, someone approached me asking very specific questions about financial planning for parents of mentally ill adult children. They knew I was a financial planner. Even though, at that point, I didn't feel like a specialist in special-needs planning, I was determined to help. That conversation, that client, became the impetus for me to learn all I could, to fill in the gaps and gain a deeper understanding of how the financial plan is affected by a serious mental illness. Every client since has been another opportunity to help people in a tough situation do better, and everywhere I go, someone else in the mental health community has another question for me about finances.

My focus for many years has been on investment philosophies and the best ways to efficiently capture returns in capital markets. Those approaches can absolutely help in the case of parents with mentally ill children. When you introduce more efficiency to a portfolio, you increase the probability the money will last longer and do more. However, an efficient investment portfolio isn't enough on its own for families dealing with the financial side of mental illness. Tackling the challenges of supporting your child with severe mental illness begins with knowledge—knowledge kills fear and drives action. Along with fighting stigma and telling our stories, building our knowledge is the most important thing we can do.

The costs of diagnosing and treating mental illness can snowball and derail your retirement plans. It's natural to prioritize your child's health over anything else, but it means you often are taking the focus off your finances at the worst possible moment. By sharing my knowledge, however, I'd like to help you be proactive and set up a plan as soon after diagnosis as possible, or to help you recover and move forward if you've overspent.

I've heard the stories of other parents' fear, confusion, frustration, and debt. I've been there too. Considering how hard it was for me to find some of these answers—and again, I'm a financial planner!—I knew we had to do better. There's a void of information and guidance out there on this important topic, and I want to share my financial planning expertise—together with my own family's experience and the experience of others—to help address that void.

## THIS BOOK IS FOR YOU

I wrote this book to be the personal-crisis intervention team for your financial plan. I'll give you a guide on how to think about money in this specific situation, and I'll offer as much hope and encouragement as I can along the way. You are not alone! So much about dealing with mental illness is confusing and worrying—finances shouldn't have to be, too.

In the following pages, I'll give you insights and tools to help you better understand (1) where you are and (2) the decisions you'll need to make to get where you want to be financially. We'll talk about how we plan for the ongoing and future needs of your mentally ill child, and how to safeguard your own financial future into retirement. I'll provide clear and direct explanations of what to do and what not to do to help you make the best possible decisions for your family's future.

But most of all, I hope I'll provide encouragement and hope. The mental illness diagnosis created chaos in your life, raising one set of challenges and concerns after another—including financial ones. Implementing the strategies and tools I'll give you will calm down the financial piece and free you up to handle the rest, bringing you more peace of mind and financial security for your family.

—

# PART ONE

# FINANCIAL CONCERNS AND CHALLENGES FACED BY PARENTS

___

# CHAPTER ONE

# The Unique Financial Landscape after Mental Illness Strikes

I first met Rachel and Doug through NAMI. Their son had been diagnosed with a severe mental illness just a few years before mine, and she and her husband were very generous with sharing their understanding.

Rachel and Doug were in a very bad spot financially. As she put it, when their son was diagnosed, their financial life started snowballing out of control. They'd bought a house at the height of the market, one just a little out of reach; when the market crashed, they were soon upside down on their mortgage. They'd taken on investments with too much risk, and in the post-2008 world, they were upside down on those, too. They'd put out a mind-blowing amount of money, as is typical, on treatments and the diagnosis process for their son. Compounding all of that, in the crisis, Doug had taken his eye off the ball at work. In his commission-based job, that suddenly meant he was bringing in significantly less income.

One decision led to another, with their mortgage and the bills for their son's treatments still coming due. There was room on a credit card, so they used it. Then another. Soon, they were deep in debt with very little real hope of getting out.

Rachel and Doug are not the only ones I've met in this situation. If someone had come to them earlier and talked to them about sound financial-planning principles, about having a cushion and a backup plan for the unexpected, maybe they wouldn't have found themselves in that situation. Instead, they simply didn't understand the risks they were taking. They had no margin for error.

The only way out of the mess Rachel and Doug were in, at that point, was bankruptcy. As tough as it is to deal with your child's mental illness, it's tougher to do it while bankrupt. I often tell this story to parents in the early stages of their child's diagnosis, as a cautionary tale. Rachel and Doug's story represents what could happen to you, so be careful it doesn't. Neither you nor your child will be helped by bankruptcy, whereas everyone can be helped if you have a sound financial plan.

## DON'T LET STIGMA STEAL FROM YOU

People are often afraid to talk about mental illness in public, afraid of what others might think or say. I've also found in my practice the more affluent a family is the less they want to disclose that a child of theirs has schizophrenia, bipolar disease, or any other serious mental illness. People who feel they have more to lose are even less willing to disclose the problem. Spending time talking to somebody about your money already feels personal, awkward, and uncomfortable. What kind of special relationship would you need with your financial advisor to talk about your child's mental illness?

I get it. Talking to a financial planner about your child's mental illness feels nearly impossible—you worry what the planner is going to think of you and your child. I've been there, embarrassed to admit I spent thousands of dollars on just one doctor visit to Vancouver, which turned out to be fruitless. It's embarrassing, so I'd rather not mention it. However, in the same way refusing to talk about mental illness means no one gets help for it, refusing to talk about the financial impact of mental illness means you can't get help for the financial side.

It's true that few financial advisors have expertise dealing with financial planning for families with adult children with mental illness. Those who've dealt with special-needs planning often specialize in children who are diagnosed with special needs when they are young, when time is on the side of the parents. It could be that the stigma hurts here, too—the planners who are comfortable planning for innocent children with a horrible disease suddenly are not comfortable with "crazy" adults. That's a shame.

I do understand it, though. As a financial planner, I hesitate telling people about my son's mental illness in a professional context as well. People seek stability in their financial planners—will they worry I will become unstable, too?

That is why, I believe, advisors have to be even more trustworthy than usual to advise people in this delicate situation. They have to be willing to go a little bit further, to question a little bit beyond what is socially acceptable, into the issues that really matter. What are your values? What are your core feelings around these very sensitive topics? Finding a financial advisor who's willing to truly know you and your family—to ask the hard questions—means the difference between generic, unhelpful advice and a meaningful plan that addresses the complex needs of a family coping with severe mental illness in an adult child.

When you've experienced the stigma of your child having psychosis in public, as I have, you get gun-shy, and you hesitate to bring up the mental illness with strangers. I understand how that could happen in your financial planner's office, too. However, I'd counsel you to find someone who truly is trustworthy, someone with whom you feel comfortable talking about these issues. Financial planners can provide a huge benefit when you need to get more out of what you have. You don't need to miss out on this benefit because of stigma.

## WHY FINANCIAL PLANNING CHANGES AFTER DIAGNOSIS

Traditional financial planning is normally focused on one goal: retirement. This is challenging enough! Planning for a future you can't see and can't control, with a market whose short-term gyrations you can't predict, and a lifetime you don't know, is all about setting yourself up for the highest probability of success you can. Hiring a financial planner with a depth of knowledge and experience can help increase your probability of achieving all that's important to you. However, trying to plan for your child's lifetime needs expands the entire landscape you're operating in and makes the job more difficult.

The planning time frame is also shortened. Other special needs often manifest at birth or soon after, so you have plenty of time to plan for your child's needs long-term. Schizophrenia and other serious mental illnesses, however, manifest in the late teens, early twenties, or later. You've been operating on one set of plans for your retirement for a long time. With this diagnosis, now you have to change those plans midstream, as quickly as you can manage, in the middle of a decade critical to the success of your retirement. Because of this shortened time frame, it can be challenging to come up with sufficient cash to fund everything you need to fund, and your health may or may not be good enough to allow you access to resources like life insurance that might help fund solutions beyond your death.

Your focus shifts from taking care of yourself to also taking care of another generation. How long will your child live? What will be required when it comes to food, shelter, and treatment costs long-term? How can you ensure your child will have access to healthcare and other benefits over the long term? Who is going to take care of your child when you're gone? Who is going to make sure your child takes medicines correctly and on time? Who will fight for your child in the medical system or in the law enforcement system? What is it all going to cost?

Because the process of diagnosis is hard with mental illness, it costs a great deal more than expected. Severe mental illness often manifests over a few years, and even the experts may not be able to understand what's going on until you're farther down the path. The emotional and physical toll is tremendous. Ideally, when you come out the other side, you will have stayed within your means or not gone hugely outside of them. Even in this best-case scenario, however, it will take some time to recover financially, and it will have impacted your long-term financial planning. Recovering emotionally from this time period also takes time. It's bewildering, upsetting, and frightening when your child develops a severe mental illness. As we've seen with Rachel and Doug's story that resulted in bankruptcy, the lack of focus on work can add its own complications.

## BE WHERE YOU ARE

Wherever you are right now, however much have you spent, and whatever impact it's had on your finances, it's best to shake off the dust of what's happened and move forward with a sensible financial plan.

For better or for worse, it seems to be very normal to spend unthinkable amounts of money in those first critical and confusing years. You wanted to do what was best for your child. If you looked at research, you saw that early intervention is best, so suddenly, any expense seemed reasonable. You prioritized your child over finances. In our search, Gayle and I found private treatment centers costing upwards of $20,000 to $30,000 per month. How can anyone but the highly affluent truly afford that? Even the places that are reasonable by comparison at $5,000 per month are still out of reach for most, and there is still no guarantee your son or daughter would be any better off by being there. Gayle and I certainly spent far more than we should have during this process. It's your instinct as a parent to do whatever is necessary for your child, so you spend and spend. All it takes is getting behind on payments to start a financial skid that can destroy even a well-structured plan.

I hope that isn't you, but if it is, take heart. If you're like Rachel and Doug, you can start with a call to a good bankruptcy lawyer. Bring it back to zero and then start over, knowing you did the best you could at the time for your child. If you're anywhere else along the road, keep reading.

My clients who are facing this situation come to me looking for reassurance that fully funding their retirement and their child's needs for their entire lifetime is possible. For many people, with careful planning, such an accomplishment *is* possible. For others, it's not—but they, too, find planning is worthwhile. It's better to make hard choices now and be comfortable with the trade-offs than to end up in a bad situation later by accident. These are difficult challenges, but they're not impossible. In the pages of this book, I'll discuss sound principles you can apply to help you know where to focus your choices and resources. I'll show you how to get the most out of what you have now and set yourself (and your family) up for the future.

Wherever you are, start today. It's never too late, but the earlier you can start, the easier the process will be.

—

# CHAPTER TWO

# Parenting the Mentally Ill in an Information Void

Firefighters are people who, against all reason, run into burning buildings instead of out of them. They can do this because they understand the principles of how fires work, allowing them to take this knowledge and apply it to smother the fire, take away its fuel, cope with deadly smoke, and carry others and themselves out of peril safely. Without an accurate understanding of how fire burns, or with a wrong understanding, many firefighters would die. Good, effective practices come from sound principles. The knowledge of fire comes first, in this case, to inform the practices of firefighting. Reality informs what it takes to be successful. Doing it the other way around is just asking for trouble.

Few investors understand this. In the world of investing, many operate on a set of principles that has little to do with academic science. All too often we see investors operate on a set of principles designed to benefit those selling investment products. Far too many investors and advisors begin with practices that sell investment products. Then, they create false principles that explain the world in a way that sells more products, while leaving investors with the same kind of mess you'd get if firefighters were trained to pour oil on fires instead of water.

Academics, on the other hand, study investing and the inner workings of markets from a perspective that tries to get at the truth of how the financial world works. Academics craft principles of reality first, and then we as investors develop practices based on those real principles. Wall Street starts with practices to benefit Wall Street and makes up principles to fit. For example, money managers famously claim they have the ability to outperform the market with better stock picking and/or market timing, while there is overwhelming academic evidence saying that just isn't so. I prefer using a set of principles that have been discovered academically rather than those crafted by Wall Street and the makers of financial products.

When you have a child with mental illness, the stakes are so much higher than they were before. You don't have the margin to waste on Wall Street's flawed ideas of the markets or to learn to navigate solely based on your instincts and personal experience. Instead, you must begin with a firm grasp of the characteristics of mental illness and its effects on financial planning. You must begin with good, sound principles.

I began with in-depth research and context for the field-at-large before focusing a large part of my firm's efforts on families who were financially affected by mental illness. I knew practices based only on one person's experience would be like Wall Street's account of the market: flawed at best, dangerous at worst. I worked to establish the first principles of how severe mental illness impacts financial planning and how those principles work out into sound practices. Now I want to pass on what I've learned to you so that you can apply these principles and practices to your situation.

## THE INFORMATION VOID

When I began looking at financial planning for mental illness, I started, as many people would, by searching online to find whatever I could on the topic. Unfortunately, there isn't much relevant information out there. Many planners focus on special needs, but I didn't find anyone working specifically with mental illness. Since the onset of severe mental illness often arrives in the late teenage years, early twenties, or later, it impacts a family's financial plan very differently than disabilities that arrive in early childhood.

I went to the sites of organizations specifically focused on mental health, such as NAMI and MHA, looking for additional information. The groups had a lot to say about important issues like services, treatment programs, and housing, but very little about the financial piece of the puzzle. I found a few outdated articles here and there, particularly from Australia and Great Britain, which had more resources than the United States, but I was appalled at how little existed in any form. Even when I went looking for specialty resources for financial planners, the information void persisted. I needed more to go on than my own experience, and I needed to know whether other families had faced challenges similar to mine. I felt frustrated and alone in trying to answer my questions, and I knew this situation had to be even more disorienting and upsetting for families who are not trained in professional money management. How do you find resources on financial planning in the case of severe mental illness if they don't exist?

## A STUDY TO FILL THE INFORMATION VOID

On the suggestion of my business coach, I conducted a study to help fill in some of the gaps in information around this topic. I began interviewing families in similar situations. My professional training is in asset management and financial planning, so I have historically worked mostly with more affluent families to manage their assets.

I focused on this group for the study as well, so I would understand how to steer others like them in the right direction when they came to work with me. The financial aspect of dealing with a family member's mental illness is hugely impactful on everyone, but the restrictions placed on disability and other programs available to those with mental illness impact those with more means in a very different way. I was determined to find out more about the financial piece of the issue of severe mental illness so I could help people plan better financially.

I approached fifteen individuals and conducted in-depth interviews with them. The interviews sometimes lasted as long as two and a half hours. I focused on a list of questions to help me understand their biggest challenges. I asked my interviewees to share their most pressing concerns, issues, and problems they faced as parents. I asked leaders of mental health organizations to share their perspectives on the most pressing concerns or issues of consumers, too.

I wanted to know what kept people up at night. I wanted to know about the major challenges they faced, specifically from a financial perspective. What mattered most? What other issues, concerns, or problems had they heard about from other parents? From there, we drilled down to financial fears.

I asked if they'd been generally successful at managing the

financial challenges associated with a child with mental illness—and why or why not. I asked them to share what they were most afraid of. The last and most important question was whether an empathetic financial planner would have been helpful, particularly early in the process. Had they met someone who clearly understood what they were going through, would it have benefitted them?

A couple of the interviewees had worked with financial planners whom they felt were specialists regarding mental health needs. Hearing this, I eagerly went back to my office and did my research. I generally found that these professionals dabbled in special-needs planning, but it wasn't their specialty, which was incredibly disappointing. A fair number of special needs attorneys write special needs trusts, but in the financial-planning field, the void in mental health-planning information on the internet mirrored at that time the void in professional expertise.

The study was incredibly helpful in understanding the issues other families were facing—and, ultimately, how I could help. Below are some key takeaways.

## LONG-TERM CARE

Without a doubt, the number-one concern of the people I interviewed was about who would take care of their mentally ill child after they passed away. Many people don't like to think about planning for their children's future after they're gone, so they wait until the last possible moment, when they're well into retirement or after they've received a dire health diagnosis. The longer you wait, however, the harder the problems become, so I'd recommend starting this process today.

Sooner or later, you'll have to come to terms with your own mortality, whether you're in your fifties—and it's only been a few years since your child was diagnosed—or you're now in your seventies with a child who still lives at home and is still, at least partially, financially dependent on you. At that point, you'll begin to worry about the future and wonder who will take care of your child—a question that goes hand in hand with where they'll live. Many children in this population do not live in institutions or assisted living facilities (ALFs); they're at home with mom and dad. Maybe they're in their forties and their parents are in their seventies—but that only makes the questions more urgent.

Caretakers also have to be advocates. In the past, when my son was hospitalized, we would go see him during his visiting hours, and we noticed that often no one shows up to visit the other patients there. It's heartbreaking. We realized they have no one in their court. Getting into specialized state-run programs and navigating the mental health bureaucracy is extremely difficult. Without advocates, who will ensure these patients are cared for adequately?

My son is in a very helpful program that serves only a fraction of the people who qualify. The program is great, but there are also communication lapses among the staff, including not making sure he has enough of his meds to last him until the next appointment. Such a mistake would have been a major problem if we hadn't caught it in time. When my son has been in the hospital, we've checked his chart and found that steps that were supposed to take place were neglected, or he's been prescribed medication that we already know from past experience has been ineffective. My son doesn't have the ability to advocate for himself as effectively as Gayle or myself, especially when he's in crisis. My wife is great about stepping in and pointing out issues on his behalf in those cases. What happens to the patients who don't have someone to push for what they need? Many people struggling with mental illness are at the mercy of the system, which doesn't always work like it's supposed to.

When parents ask, "Who will take care of my child when I'm gone?" it's about more than who pays the bills and makes sure they take their meds. The advocacy, the care, and the long-term decision-making are often just as important. Figuring out who and how is difficult. There isn't always an easy or obvious answer, but it's important to be able to go through all the possibilities and come up with a workable plan.

For some people, family is the answer. They plan for their relatives or other children to care for the child with mental illness. However, it's equally valid to want to avoid making one child sacrifice personal fulfillment in order to care for another. Furthermore, assuming family will step in may not be in the best interests of the child with special needs. People with mental illness need caretakers who have the knowledge and wherewithal to focus on them, from helping them buy toothpaste to noticing when they're on the edge of psychosis. They need to be there to help talk them down and ensure they take the appropriate medication. Other siblings may or may not be willing or able to do this, and you'll need to have hard conversations to find out.

Talking to these other parents and mental health professionals made me realize just how far we have yet to go when it comes to offering real programs that solve these problems, especially this highest-level question: "Who is going to take care of my kid when I am gone?"

## WORRIES ABOUT LAW ENFORCEMENT

Every parent I talked to had concerns about law enforcement. Will their child get shot if he gets upset at the wrong police officer? Will he be killed? Officers operate from training that doesn't always apply to people in crisis. They know how to subdue someone and take control of a situation as quickly as possible, but that's not often a good way to deal with someone in a mental health crisis. This isn't to disparage police officers—they are first responders who handle many difficult situations, but they need better and more specific training for mental illness. The fear of your child being shot in these situations is unfortunately very realistic.

We've had multiple encounters with law enforcement. It just goes with the territory. All I will share here is that the difference between working with officers with CIT training or not is like the Grand Canyon, vast and huge. In one instance, I'm pretty sure CIT training saved my son's life, and I'm immensely grateful that particular officer had gone through the training. I'm also frustrated that such training is not mandatory for all law enforcement. It's expensive to take officers out of the field and train them for a week, but as I saw, that training can mean the difference between life and death.

## FINANCIAL CHALLENGES

A mental illness diagnosis blindsides families. It changes the entire course of their finances, from retirement planning to healthcare and ongoing expenses. They face a mounting and previously unexpected burden of increased deductibles, more copays, and health-plan limitations restricting the number of times their child can receive coverage to see a mental health professional, if insurance will pay at all. As a result, they worry about the cost of healthcare, they worry about paying the treatment bills, and some worry about running out of money.

Once you're past the first crisis stage, you start realizing housing is a key component of your child's long-term needs. So many areas are experiencing a housing crisis. Most people don't want an assisted living facility (ALF) in their neighborhood, and the few that are out there are often in unsafe neighborhoods. This creates a shortage. For example, in the major metropolitan area of Broward County, Florida, there are only five facilities, most with less than twenty beds, with some of the programs only three to six months long. In the area, there are more than ten thousand potential customers with serious mental illness who will need long-term care. The shortage is real and difficult to address. If parents are unable or unwilling to have their child live with them, or are planning for the future beyond their own lifetimes, housing becomes a major and expensive hurdle.

Sometimes, the tremendous financial challenges lead good people to make wrenching decisions. I knew a family who essentially cut off their daughter financially and put her in an ALF where I would not have felt comfortable leaving my son. However, they realized if they continued on their current course, they were going to go bankrupt. They needed to preserve their finances and plan for two generations—theirs as well as hers after they were gone. A bankruptcy would have made that impossible.

Government-provided benefits can help alleviate some, but not all, of the tremendous financial pressure, but they're not easy to navigate. Parents need help navigating the system, including identifying what is available, determining their child's eligibility, and avoiding making missteps that will jeopardize benefits. Unfortunately, I've seen a lot of misinformation circulating on these topics, even at official seminars through mental health groups. Trusts and other financial instruments only add one more layer of complexity, with all the difficulties of finding and keeping a trustee or appointed guardian who really will keep the best interests of your child at heart. When I talked to parents in the survey, they felt overwhelmed when it came to government benefits and trusts and wanted help navigating them.

## RATE OF SUCCESS

I asked the parents in the survey how successful they felt they'd been in dealing with the financial aspects of mental illness. Answers varied widely, with success or failure hinging on families' financial status and how proactive they were. For instance, my family has been very fortunate—we have a relatively high income, so we have the resources to deal with issues and pursue options many other people can't. In addition, my wife strongly advocates for our son and is very proactive. Most people we talked to, however, didn't feel they were succeeding in the face of their challenges. They felt overwhelmed and lost. They often had more limited income, narrowing their options. They didn't know the tools available, and they often weren't proactive to go find them.

The good news is that some of the information families need can easily be found on the internet, if they're willing to look for it. (Government benefits information is a great example.) Some aspects of dealing with financial challenges and planning for the future under these circumstances, however, require professional advice, and the stigma around mental illness in this country can make parents reluctant to seek that advice. They fear what a financial advisor will think of them. They fear admitting that their child is struggling and that they themselves need help.

## POTENTIAL BENEFITS OF A FINANCIAL PLANNER

I asked the interviewees how a financial planner could have helped them, and the word I heard most frequently was "empathy." They wanted someone to help them slow down and think through the situation systematically. Most of the survey participants felt that input early on would have been the most helpful. An empathetic partner in the process could have helped them identify available tools, appropriate legal steps, and other professionals to talk to in the process. A good advisor would have their best interests in mind, help them examine the ramifications of their financial plans, and help them make informed decisions. Most parents in the study didn't know a financial planner with a high level of empathy for and experience with the mental illness community specifically, but they wished they did.

One of the people I spoke to emphasized how much time he could have saved if someone had connected him with the right network of professionals, such as an attorney experienced with writing a special needs trust. At my firm, we have a network of attorneys we work with who will spend hours with clients to get a deep understanding of their situation, and who will collaborate with us as a unified team for the client's best interests. I brief the attorney on everything I've learned about a potential client, so they go into their meetings deeply informed.

When it comes to considering the question of who will take care of your child when you're gone, having an advisor who has genuine empathy is particularly important. An empathetic advisor understands that you need to know who will take care of all the little tasks you do for your child every day. He or she won't give a perfunctory answer about moving your child, an adult who's been living with you his whole life, to an ALF. You need someone who will help you consider the best candidates to serve as your child's trustee or guardian, not say, "We'll just use a trust service." Empathetic guidance is informed by your lived experience, rather than reciting stock answers that only look good on paper.

Many parents in this situation feel beat up, disoriented, and confused. They're mentally and physically exhausted, they haven't slept, and they're so overwhelmed, they can't decide what step to take next. That's understandable under the circumstances! I expected that clients would always want a collaborative partner to help them make their own decisions, but in this case, parents said they wanted firm, reassuring, well-informed, paternal guidance. One interviewee described wanting an advisor to tell him what to do, someone who wouldn't necessarily explain all the reasoning behind each decision but could tell him the next step with confidence. For him, a strong, reassuring answer was a concrete next step. When people are going through a family crisis, they don't always have the bandwidth to consider the decision-making process; they want someone trustworthy to simply tell them what action to take. That was surprising to me, but I was happy to know what would be helpful.

This book can't entirely fill the trusted advisor role, because I don't know the specific details of your particular situation. Even so, I hope it can point you in the right direction. Get as far as you can on your own, and then consider working directly with an empathetic, knowledgeable advisor. He or she can spend at least a couple of hours with you, learn the intricacies of your situation, and come up with a plan including direct steps to take (if that's the relationship you're looking for). When I speak to a client about the right next steps to take, I've spent hours researching and reflecting on my own as well as in conversations with collaborators in the legal, tax, and insurance fields. I have the foundation to feel confident in outlining their path to success. I'm happy to go into the reasoning and process of decision-making if it's helpful, but I don't have to. If a next step is what a client needs, I will give them the next step.

## A NARROW FOCUS

When I realized there were few professional financial planners focused on mental illness, I knew I had to step in to help fill the void. However, I worried. Was there a reason advisors weren't working in this space? Was I making a mistake? I had a thriving business working with affluent families already. Did it really make sense for me to focus time, energy, and resources on what might be a losing proposition? I worried I'd pigeonhole myself into an extremely narrow specialty—not only special needs, but mental health specifically. Fortunately, it hasn't had to be an "either/or" choice. I have enough people working for me that we can take care of a range of needs, and I can focus on this particular niche for which I know there is a great need.

What's in your heart is more important than what's in your wallet. I've pursued this work because there's a gap in knowledge that has a profound impact on people's lives. Parents of adult children with mental illness need answers. It was hard for me to find those answers, even with a very high level of financial knowledge and resources. For someone without my background, retirement planning is challenging enough; adding a mental health crisis to the financial mix would likely feel like plummeting off a cliff.

Speaking with other parents about their experience with mental illness has made it clear that people need serious help and answers to their pressing questions, and it's critical for me to help fill that information void. It's why I have written this book.

## THE EVOLUTION OF MY MISSION AND WORK

My wife and I have decided to commit our lives to doing whatever we can to help make the world a better place for families battling mental illness. We continue to work to raise awareness in the community and to address the questions and concerns that others have. We are both extremely involved in our local NAMI chapter and, as of this writing, I serve on the board as vice president.

My wife is heavily involved in the NAMI Advocacy Group. Members call themselves "NAGs," and they lobby representatives and senators at the local and state levels to allocate more money to mental health concerns, particularly housing. Her deep understanding of others' experiences has found its expression in public advocacy—she wants to change the world, and it has essentially become her full-time job.

For my part, I've also devoted my work professionally to helping people navigate the financial side of mental illness. It's much more than a job—it's a mission. Not only do I advocate for my son and work on behalf of my clients, but I also work through NAMI to figure out how we can offer more programs and services to everyone.

Our journey with mental illness as a family has inspired us to help people beyond our own family. Raising awareness and helping the community has expanded to be a focus of my work, too, and that mission has become our whole life—we strive to do something small to extend that mission every single day.

## COMPREHENSIVE FINANCIAL PLANNING

Most financial advisors aren't bad people, but they do have to make a living. Traditional financial planning is a sales-driven industry. One of the main players in the special needs space is a large, well-known life insurer, with about eight hundred planners nationwide. The reality is, at the end of the day, despite their position devoted to special needs, the company's number-one objective is to make money. Ideally, they want to sell you a life insurance policy and perhaps the investments for your investment account. Regardless of good intentions, and regardless of what the client really needs, in a structure where advisors get paid for selling products, they are going to sell the products. This is what I call the "dark side" of financial planning. The hidden incentives mean that, to make money, even well-meaning advisors sell clients products that may not be the best solutions to serve their needs and might, in rare cases, even actively hurt them.

In contrast, fee-only financial planners charge a fee for their advice, either as a small percentage of the assets they manage or as a flat fee or even hourly fee. This puts the planner into a "fiduciary" relationship with the client, meaning the planner is required to do what is in the client's best interest rather than his own. When there are other noncommissioned and possibly more effective choices out there, a commissioned product with a high fee structure probably isn't in the client's best interest. Because of this, the fiduciary planner will offer (and is required by law to offer) the other, better choices, even if he or she doesn't make as much money.

At my firm, we're proudly fee-only, which makes us a fiduciary to our clients. We've taken the perspective that there are four additional key areas in which we can assist clients, beyond making smart decisions with their investments, and all four are critical.

1. **Wealth enhancement** grows and stretches the limited resources families already have as far as we can. This can include tax mitigation, decreasing debt costs, and increasing cash flow.
2. We focus on **wealth transfer** that is as efficient as possible, plays by the rules, and in the case of children with mental illness or other disabilities, maintains eligibility for critical government benefits.
3. Effective **wealth protection** strategies ensure clients protect their assets without worrying about losing it all in a lawsuit resulting from their child's conduct or whatever unexpected circumstances life brings.
4. Finally, **charitable giving** complements the other pieces while advancing a client's legacy and values.

Northstar Financial Planners offers a comprehensive service in which investment consulting is just one piece of the larger picture. Many clients come to us concerned about the mental illness diagnosis and wanting to make better financial decisions. We help them with that, but we also show them there's more to an effective financial plan than investing assets in a particular way. A truly effective plan looks at resources comprehensively to get the most from every dollar to support parents and their children. Families need someone empathetic who will take the extra step to say, "Listen, I recommend you meet with this attorney," and explain to you why it is in your best interest. A well-intentioned advisor whose compensation ends after selling a product has little reason to take those extra steps that are so critical in the case of families coping with mental illness.

## THERE IS HOPE

The problems you're facing aren't easy, and they aren't ones that traditional financial planning alone is built to solve. That doesn't mean you can't solve them! Spend the time to find out what your options are, and think deeply about the decisions you'll need to make. So many people are already fighting for more solutions, housing, and legislation benefitting those with mental illness, and they are often winning. Since the landscape is changing so rapidly, however, you'll need to be plugged into your community to know what resources are available and how to help. I'll offer specific financial solutions and resources in the following pages, but your best and most current information will come from those in the community around you.

Knowledge is power, and community is key.

---

# PART TWO

# FINANCIAL PLANNING STRATEGIES AND TOOLS FOR PARENTS

# CHAPTER THREE

---

# A Primer on Government Benefits: Social Security and Medicaid

Government benefits are a cornerstone of a viable financial plan for a child with mental illness, but navigating the process can be challenging. In this chapter, I walk you through the basic information you need both to apply for and to retain the benefits for which your child is eligible.

## MY FAMILY'S EXPERIENCE

Many people struggle with the idea of receiving government benefits. They may feel that there's a stigma attached or assume if they're making a good income, they're not the intended recipients. They don't always see these benefits are, for the most part, earned benefits, like retirement income, and not a handout. In my family's case, it never occurred to us to apply. One day, however, the leader of a NAMI support group told my wife Gayle she'd be thankful later if she applied now. Gayle went online and got the list of everything that we'd need, and then she took all the documentation to the Social Security office. Based on that experience, I would say the more information you have about your child's situation and history, the better you'll be able to make your case to the Social Security representative and the easier your experience will be. If you only come in with a little bit of documentation, the process will be arduous, because you'll have to come back with paperwork from the doctor and other proof of your situation. If you bring in a stack of documents spelling out your child's exact circumstances, the officer will be impressed, and the process will proceed much more smoothly.

Before long, we were done with the application process, and monthly benefit checks started showing up in my son's account.


## PREPARATION IS KEY

You can apply for benefits online at SSA.gov or call 1-800-772-1213 to make an in-office or telephone appointment. Either way, be sure to visit the website first and review the application checklist. Items you'll need include your child's birth certificate, proof of citizenship, documentation of marriage or military service, if applicable, and complete medical history, including any hospitalizations. You can't bring too much information—more is better. The website is easy reading in straightforward language, and I'd recommend studying it.

People with severe mental illness are eligible for benefits if they meet the Social Security definition of a disability: something that has caused someone to lose the ability to gain substantial employment. SSA.gov/disability has a list spelling out the applicable criteria exactly, and there are certain diagnoses that essentially ensure the application will be approved, including the schizophrenia spectrum and certain kinds of bipolar disorder.

I've met a few families whose initial application was denied. Typically, there was a question about their child's diagnosis as well as incomplete paperwork, but in some cases, they were able to appeal later in the process, when they had more paperwork evidence. Just like any other disabling situation, if a person is on the cusp, there might be some difficulty in meeting the Social Security definition of disability. For the most part, though, the people we've met through NAMI have had few problems with their applications. So if you think your child may qualify, go ahead and apply. There's no reason not to try, and the benefits can make a big difference.

## KEY BENEFITS

There are several benefits that can apply to a family with a mentally ill child: SSI, SSDI, and Medicaid.

## SSI AND SSDI

There are two key income benefits to be aware of: Supplemental Security Income (SSI) and Social Security Disability Insurance (SSDI). Both are ongoing income streams that can be available to your child for as long as they are disabled.

SSDI is for insured workers, meaning that they've worked long enough and paid Social Security taxes. Qualifying for SSDI requires a work history, and children under eighteen draw from their parents' benefits. For instance, I have a client whose brother is in his late fifties and has been receiving SSDI since he was seventeen. He's on their father's benefits, even though the father passed away long ago. In many cases, SSDI pays more than SSI, so if your child is a minor and meets the criteria, you should consider applying to see if they can receive SSDI. If your child is diagnosed late enough in life to have been working in a regular job and paying Social Security through the system, similarly, he or she is eligible for SSDI through his or her own account.

On the other hand, SSI is purely based on financial need.

People who qualify draw from the Social Security system even though they've never had a job to contribute to it. The payments are normally smaller than the ones through SSDI, so if you qualify for SSDI, you may be better off.

## MEDICAID

Medicaid is health insurance jointly funded by the state and federal governments. It's a benefit designed specifically for people with low incomes or special needs, from kids to elderly people and from visual impairment to severe mental illness—anyone with a disability meeting the Social Security definition is eligible. The program is offered through the federal government, but the exact eligibility definitions vary from state to state. As of this writing, in about thirty-three states and the District of Columbia, if you're eligible for SSI, you're automatically eligible for Medicaid as well, without having to fill out an additional application. That was my son's situation in Florida: soon after receiving SSI, he was enrolled in the Medicaid program as well. In other states, you still have to qualify for SSI, but then you need to fill out an additional application to qualify for Medicaid.

Even if you have private insurance, I'd highly recommend signing your child up for Medicaid. The excellent program my son is currently enrolled in is funded completely by Medicaid, and without it, he would not have been eligible.

## SSI AND SSDI IN-DEPTH

SSI and SSDI are two different government programs that provide an income stream to people who meet the Social Security definition of disabled. There are special rules that make it possible for people receiving SSDI benefits and SSI to work and still receive monthly payments. However, SSDI and SSI have different rules, so you will want to be sure you understand what the rules are in your state. An excellent publication (*Working While Disabled: How We Can Help*) that talks about earnings and Social Security benefits is available on the ssa.gov website.

As I described previously, SSDI is for people who previously worked or who were under eighteen when they first became eligible and claimed benefits under a parent's account. SSI is for people who have never worked and don't have a Social Security account. Those eligible to receive SSI can receive a monthly maximum benefit of $750 for an eligible individual or $1,125 for an eligible individual with an eligible spouse (2018), and continue doing so as long as they remain eligible.

Income is counted against the maximum SSI benefit, including in-kind support. For instance, if your child lives with you, but you do not charge rent, then the in-kind support of that living arrangement will be deducted from the benefit. If the value of the living expense is calculated at $250, then that would be subtracted from the maximum of

$750, and your child living rent-free would only receive a monthly benefit of $500. Many parents don't think about in-kind support, but it can have a big impact on benefits. After about six months of our son being on SSI, my wife and I received some sound advice from the Social Security office: if we charged our son rent and could provide proof of a monthly draft from his bank account into ours, he would be eligible for the full benefit. That's what we did, and I would advise you to do the same. Realize you must have proof. The office actually does check, and your records will be audited periodically.

If you have guardianship over your child, then you'll have a say in how the benefits are spent. In our son's case, he has the cognitive ability and has demonstrated that he will be responsible with the money in his account. (We are careful not to let it accumulate above $2,000, which I will discuss in more detail below.) He spends enough money on personal items and food that it doesn't normally accumulate, but we keep an eye on the account just in case.

SSDI may provide more substantial benefits depending on how long the recipient worked, what their wages were, or whether they're drawing on a parent's benefits. Just as in retirement, some people receive larger Social Security checks than others, depending on their work history.

## FACTORS THAT MAY REDUCE BENEFITS

There are a number of situations that may reduce benefits or eliminate them altogether, and it's important for families to understand the rules to avoid financial missteps that could negatively impact their child's eligibility.

There are certain kinds of property a recipient can have that are considered noncash assets. For instance, the recipient is usually allowed to own a car, as they may need it for transportation—but they can't have two cars. They can also have a house in their name, provided it's where they live. Additionally, having a small life insurance policy (less than $1,500) and a burial plot or burial funds (again, less than $1,500) is also acceptable while receiving SSI.

The important thing to watch is cash assets. Recipients aren't allowed to have more than $2,000 in investments or any additional assets beyond those mentioned above. This is why I mentioned that we're careful not to let my son's bank account accumulate more than that amount. SSA.gov has a lot of helpful information on this issue. You can type your questions into the search box, or you can use your search engine to find the pages on the SSA website that you need as well as other relevant articles.

Families have to be extremely careful not to exceed that $2,000 threshold. If my son's checking account were to go over $2,000, I would want to make sure the money got out of there immediately—the same day—or his SSI benefits would be in jeopardy. People often get into trouble with gifts. Many affluent people use gifts as an estate-planning tool. They send checks to their younger relatives, usually toward the end of the year, in the maximum gift exclusion amount, which is currently $15,000 (2018). If my son received a check like that, we could not let him cash it. We'd have to return it, because cashing it would mean he would be well over the $2,000 limit, and it would be the end of his SSI benefits. The same is true of life insurance payouts or other inheritance. If parents aren't aware of these issues, they can inadvertently jeopardize their child's benefits. This is why ABLE accounts and special needs trusts offer so much value, which I'll discuss in later chapters. You can provide for your child while taking advantage of financial instruments that don't disqualify your child from government benefits.

Before applying for SSI or SSDI on your child's behalf, it's important to verify they aren't the beneficiary of any other cash assets, including college funds. If they are, the money will need to be rolled over into an ABLE account (we'll discuss this more later), or the beneficiary should be changed to a different family member. If your child's assets do go over $2,000, they will not lose benefits forever, but they won't receive them until their assets drop below that threshold. For instance, if your child's bank account were to rise to anything above $2,000, you may find their benefits have ceased. When you apply for benefits, you also are giving Social Security the ability to monitor your child's accounts electronically. They will know. When the amount drops below the limit again, you may want to notify the office that your child is now eligible again.

As I discussed previously, in-kind support reduces benefits, including rent-free housing. So does a documented allowance or other financial support. If you're charging your child rent, as described above, the documentation can be as simple as showing a draft from their account into your account every month. Note that the account cannot be jointly owned by you and your child—the two have to be separate, and the money has to go from one to the other.

## MEDICAID IN-DEPTH

Medicaid follows the same disability definition as SSI and SSDI. In order to qualify for Medicaid, a person first has to be eligible for one of those two benefits. In the majority of states, once people receive SSI or SSDI, they're automatically enrolled in Medicaid. In the other states, you have to be more proactive to find out which extra paperwork you need to submit.

The SSA.gov website lists which states have automatic enrollment and which require an additional application as well as other eligibility requirements. I haven't done business in every state—and legislation changes over time—so do your research online to find the most up-to-date information about specific eligibility requirements applying to your jurisdiction.

As with SSI and SSDI, Medicaid recipients are currently limited to $2,000 in cash assets. One caveat to this is if a recipient is the owner of an ABLE account. As you'll see in chapter 6, ABLE account owners can still retain SSI and SSDI benefits as long as their ABLE account value is less than $100,000. However, a person with $100,000 or more in an ABLE account is still eligible for health insurance through Medicaid.

## MEDICAID AND OTHER HEALTH INSURANCE

For some people, private insurance or an employer-paid plan may be an option. For example, if an employer's health insurance plan covers dependents, you can usually add your son or daughter to your plan up to the age of twenty-six. But check with your employer or your plan. Some states and plans have different rules. However, private insurance shouldn't necessarily preclude you from applying for Medicaid as well. I recommend that all families get Medicaid coverage if their son or daughter qualifies, because it's a free government benefit that can reduce out-of-pocket expenses and increase the healthcare choices available to their children. In my son's case, my business has good benefits, and he's covered with great health insurance through that plan. But because the private plan has deductibles and copays, we don't use it for everything. He sees a psychiatrist through a Medicaid program, and we also use the government coverage for his medications.

As with SSI and SSDI, some people may feel there is a stigma attached to receiving Medicaid or be resistant to receiving help from the government. It's true that Medicaid is a government benefit, and you hear the word tossed around a lot during election seasons. In my family's case, it hadn't ever occurred to us that government-funded insurance was something our child might need or be eligible for. However, the coverage is free and, more importantly, gives him access to needed services. He's in a great program right now that he can only access by being qualified for SSI. So, we're giving him the best opportunities we can by ensuring he remains eligible for government benefits and stays in the Medicaid program. I encourage other families, regardless of their level of affluence, to look into these options, too.

## CHILDREN OVER TWENTY-SIX

Under current insurance rules, in most cases, children can be covered on their parents' health plans until they turn age twenty-six—but after that, they're on their own, regardless of disability status. So even if you have good private insurance and robust savings, your child will still need health insurance once they age out of your plan. Getting them enrolled in Medicaid as soon as they're eligible ensures a smooth transition and consistent coverage while making the most of the financial resources available for their care. As I mentioned, it's not only about saving money, but it's also about having access to important services and benefits.

## OTHER BENEFITS FOR PEOPLE MEETING THE SOCIAL SECURITY DEFINITION OF DISABILITY

If you are receiving SSI or SSDI benefits, you may be eligible for the Supplemental Nutrition Assistance Program (SNAP) as well. This is the program often referred to as "food stamps." You can learn all about SNAP at www.fns. usda.gov/snap. The reason this may be important to you, especially if your son or daughter is at home with you, is that technically feeding your son or daughter who is receiving SSI or SSDI benefits is an in-kind benefit and could *reduce* your child's benefit by a like amount that Social Security feels you are paying to feed him or her. In our case, we were advised by a Social Security representative to apply, and it was good information.

## THE BOTTOM LINE: JUST APPLY

Like the NAMI group leader told my wife: go ahead and

apply for SSI or SSDI and Medicaid—you'll thank me later. Of course, some people have religious or ethical objections to certain financial decisions, whether it's carrying debt of any kind or receiving government benefits. If that's your situation, you should, of course, make your own decision accordingly. If you don't have objections on principle, however, I would counsel you to apply for SSDI or SSI and Medicaid for your child sooner rather than later. It's money that people with disabilities are entitled to as Americans, regardless of their family's financial status, and I do not recommend leaving that money on the table. Additionally, and perhaps more importantly, participating in SSI or SSDI and Medicaid may make your child qualify for programs you wouldn't be able to qualify for without it. If you're not sure where to start, make an appointment at the Social Security office—the people who work there are on your side, and they'll help you through every step of the process.

At every NAMI meeting, someone asks whether they should apply for government benefits, and everyone else as a unit answers with an unequivocal yes. Just do it. You'll thank me later.

---

# CHAPTER FOUR

# Have a Systematic Plan

There's a saying that goes, "If you fail to plan, you are planning to fail." I'd go one further on that and say, "If you don't have a plan, you've already failed. It'll just take some time for it to be obvious to you and everyone else."

Imagine the sense of well-being you'll feel with a well-thought-out, well-designed plan. A good plan has a high probability of success yet fits your individual life, your goals, and your objectives. It's a plan that details what to do and why you are doing it, with every piece in that plan designed to serve a purpose toward your goals. Unfortunately, most people don't have such a plan—at best the plan they have is cobbled together, made up as they go. In the unlikely event it succeeds, it's by luck and accident, but far too often, its failure is inevitable.

Wouldn't you rather plan for success?

## THE TYPICAL, COBBLED-TOGETHER FINANCIAL PLAN

Very few people start their adult life with an organized plan to meet clearly defined financial goals and objectives. They might have heard they should take advantage of their employer's 401(k) match, so they contribute 3 percent to their account or whatever the maximum match is. I've just described the extent of the typical person's retirement planning. People often neglect to ask themselves how much they'll actually need to retire, what quality of life they want to have, how much they would have to contribute to get there, what they can expect from Social Security, and so on.

I have a client I'll call Tammy, who is in her late sixties and had money from previous 401(k)s sitting in a couple of different individual retirement accounts (IRAs). All the money was in cash because she really didn't understand the stock market, and it made her nervous. What she didn't understand was that these assets were actually losing purchasing power year after year because the interest she was earning was less than the rate of inflation. She had also sold some real estate a few years earlier, and the proceeds from that were sitting in cash in a bank account, so that money was losing purchasing power, too. It's like she was being financially strangled to death, so slowly that it would be a decade before she realized that she was doomed. But by then, it would have been too late.

Tammy has a son and a daughter, and both were listed as beneficiaries on her IRAs as well as on a life insurance policy. Her daughter was in her forties and had special needs because of mental illness. Tammy didn't realize, if she died, all the money her daughter inherited from her would destroy her daughter's eligibility for government benefits.

Tammy's situation is extremely typical. In the face of pressing mental health challenges, who has time to think about financial details like IRA and life insurance beneficiaries? She was worried about getting her daughter's medication, where she was going to live, and other pressing issues—not about long-term estate strategies.

Tammy hadn't done any estate planning. She was astute enough to have set up a life estate for her son, which is a great way to pass real estate on to the next generation. Her son essentially owned the house without being able to sell it or force Tammy out of it as long as she was alive. However, the life estate was the extent of her arrangements. She didn't have a will! She lacked other important estate-planning documents like a durable power of attorney or a healthcare surrogate, so there was no plan in place if she became unable to function or make decisions on her own.

She had essentially no long-term financial plan in place, particularly regarding her daughter with special needs. When she died, she didn't know what would happen to her daughter or to her Medicaid and SSI benefits. She sensed her situation might be a mess, and she needed guidance.

Tammy's situation was a problem because she'd cobbled her financial plan together over time without a clear plan. She had objectives that were extremely important to her, such as ensuring the well-being of her daughter. Due to the lack of overarching focus or a plan driving her decisions, however, she was unlikely to succeed in meeting her goals. Some of the steps she'd taken were actually undermining them!

Start by assessing where you are starting from and where you want to go. When my firm works with a new client, we start with a discovery process to outline what their goals are, what their values are, who their most important relationships are with, and what assets they have. We then use that information—and our knowledge of their current financial arrangements—to show them the probability they'll succeed in their objectives if they stick to their current path. We run up to one thousand different investment scenarios based on historical outcomes in the markets, randomly mixing returns from many decades of global stock and bond markets going up, down, or staying stagnant to different degrees. Examining these scenarios allows us to determine the probability of success.

In Tammy's case, we ran the numbers, and she statistically had a 95 percent chance of failure. In other words, she was virtually guaranteed to fail over her lifetime. After we had worked with her on a financial plan and the steps to reach it, we were able to significantly increase her probability that she won't run out of money in her lifetime. She had peace of mind and felt confident in her future for the first time in years.

For some clients, it may not be possible to hit as high a probability of success as Tammy did. Even so, it's still better to get a realistic picture of their situation and then prioritize for better outcomes. Sometimes, increasing the likelihood of success means making hard choices and sacrifices. If a family has limited assets, the trip to Italy on their bucket list won't happen once we prioritize—because if it did, it would mean sacrificing the future security of their child, which they consider far more important.

Even though denial can be tempting, it's better to go through the pain of those realizations now and plan for them than to procrastinate and end up in a worse situation. Dealing with financial problems is like addressing tooth decay. You might not want to go to the dentist right now because you're afraid it's going to hurt. However, if you go now and deal with the decay as it is, you'll avoid a lot more pain down the road. You'll get to keep your teeth for the rest of your life instead of losing them because you wanted to avoid the short-term discomfort. Similarly, it's better to face the discomfort of sharing your financial statements and bank accounts with a trustworthy professional now, to ask hard questions and face reality as it is, than to end up dealing with a desperate financial situation later through lack of planning.

## A SYSTEMATIC PLAN

I can't prescribe the best plan for your particular situation without meeting you, because good financial planning isn't one-size-fits-all. Every family is different, and every family wants something different from life, so everyone's best plan is truly unique. I hope you'll come away from this chapter understanding that you need an intentional plan and how you can get started creating one.

The most important thing is not to default to a cobbled-together status quo. Like it did for Tammy, more often than not, a default plan generally means failure to achieve your goals, unless by chance you already have more money than you could possibly spend or you win the lottery. However, we all hear many stories of people who win a lottery and go bankrupt in just a few short years. Even people who didn't gain their wealth from a windfall will fail if they outstrip their means or live beyond their money through an excessive lifestyle. In that way, financial planning really can mean life or death. Plan to succeed, because failing to plan means planning to fail.

## SETTING FINANCIAL GOALS FOR TWO GENERATIONS

Crafting a successful financial plan, whether you're doing it yourself or working with a professional advisor, starts by deciding what you want. Your objectives can change over time, but there needs to be a primary goal or priority to organize around starting now. Otherwise, you'll just be following your nose, stringing practices together instead of building from relevant principles. Once you know what you want—once you have a goal—you can figure out what the best way is to achieve that goal.

Creating a systematic financial plan is not easy. Having a child with mental illness adds an extra layer of challenge and complexity to an already difficult task. My initial reaction to tackling my family's finances in light of my son's diagnosis was shock. For my whole adult life, I thought I only had to raise my kids and get them started in their lives as self-supporting adults. I figured my wife and I would enjoy a nice, comfortable lifestyle at that point, with our assets only having to support us until we died. My son's mental illness has changed that picture entirely. Whereas some people worry about having enough money to last them until they die, we now have to think about having enough money to last until our *son* dies. What if he lives into his eighties and needs support his entire life? His financial security will require careful planning, planning for two generations.

Some parents do divorce their assets from their children with mental illness and leave the future up to SSI or SSDI and Medicaid. In particular, parents with fewer assets may take the stance that unless the government covers something, their child will simply have to go without. In my experience, more affluent families put great emphasis on ensuring their child's quality of life remains higher than a government-defined subsistence level, as expensive as that value is. The question then becomes how to stretch assets as far as they can go by increasing efficiency and using all available financial tools.

If planning for two lifetimes feels daunting to you, you're not alone. Most people feel overwhelmed simply planning for their own retirement in this age of increased life expectancies. When you add the question of planning for your child's entire adult future, most people will break out in a cold sweat. You love your child and want the best for them, so it's natural to worry about your ability to provide for them and to fear failing them financially. I feel determined not to let my son end up on the street. Fortunately, there are concrete steps we can all take to make the most of our assets and increase the chances of success for ourselves *and* our children.

Your life and your child's life may not be all you need to think about, however. There may be other family members to consider, too. For instance, I also have a daughter, and she isn't struggling with mental illness. Is it fair for me to direct the majority of our estate toward my son over his lifetime and leave her nothing? Families need to consider how to allocate their assets in a way that aligns with their values and their priorities, particularly if they have multiple children. Parents need to have conversations with their children without special needs. As the healthy children get older, particularly if they find financial success on their own, they may feel fine about all or most of their parents' estate going to a sibling with mental illness. The important step is to consider the financial situation from all angles and choose the path that most closely aligns with the family's priorities.

## THE COMPENSATION MODEL MATTERS

Professional planners help uncover the specific strengths and weaknesses of each individual's situation, and that process is valuable. If you decide that you'd be better off creating a financial plan with a professional planner, then it's important to understand how the planner is compensated. This one detail can have an outsized impact on your plan's potential success.

The financial-planning industry has grown, evolved, and

improved over the course of my career. I believe the vast majority of planners genuinely want to help people. The problem lies in the inherent conflict of interest between wanting to do right by clients and getting paid on commission. If you meet with a prospective planner, the first question you should ask is how they get paid. If they get paid *any portion* of their compensation by selling you a life insurance policy, an annuity, commissions from investment sales, or some other financial instrument, then there is an inherent conflict of interest between you and that planner, and it's difficult to imagine they could have your best interest above their own. You need someone who will instead work *for you* on a fiduciary level.

I've had a long career as a financial planner, and I've seen all sides of the compensation model question. I've been (1) a commissioned advisor and (2) a "fee-based" advisor who had the ability to charge a fee for part of the planning *and* receive commissions from product sales on the other part, and (3) I'm currently a fee-only full fiduciary advisor. That represents a lot of years of learning and striving to do what's right for my clients. My current compensation model reflects that journey to put my clients' needs first.

You want a planner who works for you and not for the company who employs them to sell products. I can't stress that enough.

The compensation model guides the planner and ultimately defines the process. At the beginning of my career, it was actually called the "sales process." I was taught early in my career how to guide my client toward the ultimate destination we (the company that employed me, and I) sought, which was the sale of a product. Whether it was a life insurance policy, a mutual fund, an annuity, or all of the above, every step in the process was designed to end in a transaction—and as quickly as possible.

Since the process is transaction-oriented and designed to accommodate as many people as possible, advisors in this world are not trained, nor do they have any interest, in going deep. Finding out the motivations and reasons behind the goals takes precious time. Few advisors are taught effective techniques for discovering their clients' real values or to find out what drives them and what's truly most important to them.

Working under a compensation model that involves commissions isn't in the best interest of any client, but it can be particularly detrimental in the case of planning for a family with a child with mental illness. To account for special needs, there are essential questions to ask and steps to take, and some of those steps don't have a commission built in. As a result, certain vital aspects of creating a sound financial plan for the family probably won't come up at all in a sales-driven setting, which is a scary thought.

Planners focus on the primary goals of getting their clients to retirement and helping them have sufficient assets to last until death. Planning for the entire life of a dependent adult child adds additional challenges—challenges that go beyond the typical planner's experience. This chapter spells out some of the things you need to consider in order to fill in the gaps to meet those new challenges.

## A BETTER EXPERIENCE

I'll walk you through the process I take with my clients and cover the issues you should definitely have on your radar. That being said, this is not a how-to guide. The specifics of your plan must come from careful consideration of your unique situation. Everyone's financial picture and goals are different. In my practice, we follow a highly consultative process to understand each family's particular goals and resources. I will give an overview of that process, but you'll need to seek out the details applicable to your needs.

## THE WEALTH MANAGEMENT FORMULA

I think of the wealth management process as a formula:

$$WM = IC + AP + RM$$

What does that mean in practice? Complete wealth management is made up of the sum of investment consulting, advanced planning, and relationship management.

## INVESTMENT CONSULTING (IC)

The first key area of this holistic approach is investment consulting. First and foremost, clients with assets want to make smart decisions about their money. They come to us wanting to know about the best investment options available to them given their situation and the current economy. Clients want to know how they should structure their investments to most efficiently reach their goals and achieve all that is important to them. Investment guidance is the most fundamental service offered by financial planners, and we can safely assume 100 percent of financial planners offer this advice, some better than others.

## ADVANCED PLANNING (AP)

Investment consulting alone isn't enough. I'd argue it's really just table stakes—the minimal starting point to get a seat at the table. Beyond investment consulting, clients need four key concerns to be addressed and regularly reviewed for a plan to be effective. These four concerns become the cornerstones of the Advanced Plan. The intention of advanced planning is to ensure your entire house is in order, not just the investment component. The primary categories of advanced planning are wealth enhancement, wealth transfer, wealth preservation, and charitable giving.

### Wealth Enhancement

Wealth enhancement practices include mitigating your taxes, decreasing debt costs, and increasing income. Here, you answer questions such as these: How do I get more out of the money that I have and make it last longer, based on my current level of income and my current investments? How do I decrease my debt costs? How do I increase my cash flows? How do I mitigate my taxes more effectively? Taxes are often the key aspect in this area: putting to work knowledge of IRS rules to increase the amount of money you can put toward your goals.

### Wealth Transfer

Wealth transfer concerns often represent the most important part of the holistic financial plan for clients dealing with special needs such as mental illness. The primary focus is on how to transfer your estate as efficiently as possible and to meet your desires along the way. For families with special needs, we must pay careful attention to ensure valuable government benefits and programs are not jeopardized. For families with multiple children, there can also be questions of parity—given the assets in the estate and the needs of the child with mental illness, how can we "even" things up to make inheritance as fair as possible for the other children as well?

As we're looking at estate issues, it's also important to address issues that may arise when life takes a turn for the worse. We'll need to assemble basic documents such as a durable power of attorney and healthcare surrogate forms. These transfer important decision-making powers to someone else in the event you aren't able to make decisions yourself. As we'll talk about in more depth later, special needs trusts are an important tool for estate planning and wealth transfer for families facing severe mental illness concerns, and should be considered within the larger picture of your needs in this area.

### Wealth Protection

Everyone has some level of concern that they could fall prey to someone taking their money, perhaps through an unexpected lawsuit. We've found that as people become more affluent, these concerns tend to increase, as you feel you have more to lose. Your worries might include the possibility of being sued because of something your child with mental illness does. We work with our clients to build wealth protection strategies to ensure assets are titled correctly. We set up appropriate kinds and amounts of insurance, put a good risk-management program in place, and pay attention to cybersecurity. Then, we look at best practices for managing your accounts so that you can protect the wealth you've accumulated and use it efficiently in service of your plan's other areas.

### Charitable Giving

For clients who want to direct some of their wealth toward the goal of making the world a better place, charitable giving becomes an essential part of the plan. Such giving can also help with other areas, including tax mitigation. Unfortunately, it's very common to need to scale back or sacrifice the giving element of a plan because of the increased costs associated with caring for a child with mental illness. It's also common for families dealing with special needs to be less affluent for interrelated reasons, including the increased stress leading to higher rates of divorce. Not everyone includes charitable giving, but when they do, it becomes an important component of the Advanced Plan.

## RELATIONSHIP MANAGEMENT (RM)

The final component of the wealth management formula is relationship management, which for our firm encompasses both client relationship management and professional network or expert relationship management.

On the client relationship side, the wealth manager oversees all the essential steps of the process and works with the client to keep them on track. Rather than leave the client on his or her own, management ensures the client can make the most out of their time and money, allowing them to get closer to their goals and enjoy life more. The wealth manager ensures the client continues moving in the right direction, often by taking tasks off the client's plate entirely.

The professional network side involves ensuring we have a team of experts who are all on the same page and working together to help implement the client's plan. These experts include tax advisors, lawyers, insurance representatives, and other professionals who are key to achieving the client's objectives. If your current professionals aren't working for you, then as your wealth manager, I would either get them on board or refer you to experts who will be a better fit. I work to coordinate the whole team cohesively and ensure there is a master plan all the members understand and are committed to.

If you are developing a financial plan on your own, then you'll need to identify the types of professionals who are essential to your team, establish relationships with them, and keep them coordinated and moving toward your goals.

## PUTTING IT ALL TOGETHER

To give you an idea of how my firm ties all this together,

I'll briefly walk you through the process we use and the meetings we conduct with our clients. The process has a natural progression and is entirely focused on achieving what is most important to our clients.

## DISCOVERY

Every new client relationship begins with a deep-dive discovery. In order to really learn what is most important to our prospective client, we have to have an in-depth, comprehensive picture of their situation and priorities. It's important to know about all their assets, of course, but it's equally essential to understand who the important people in their life are and why. Who benefits from their finances? Who are the challenging people in their life from a financial perspective? Why, for example, is a client estranged from a sibling, and what part does that estrangement play in the client's goals and understanding of finances?

A great discovery process requires answering fundamental questions, some of which may seem obvious but actually aren't. We ask clients about their most important values, and ask what money means to them. The answers to those questions are different for everyone. Many say something about security, but there are so many variations in what security means to people that it's worth diving deeper to create a meaningful plan for each client. Once we have a sense of his or her underlying values, we can move on to discussing financial goals.

Something that sets my firm apart is that we don't stop at goals. We ask our clients about the achievements they're most proud of and why, and we ask them to share their bucket lists. These personal questions go beyond concrete objectives and get to the heart of our customers' passions and motivations. The conversations end up uncovering dreams they might not otherwise have mentioned, such as wanting to write a novel or pursue another passion not directly related to spending or making money. People have aspirations that are extensions of their values, and we need to understand them. Diversifying their portfolio or helping them save for a house might be beneficial, but it won't help them carve out the opportunity to be a writer before they die.

People who don't have an empathetic, personal connection with their financial planner are unlikely to maintain a long relationship because there will always be another firm out there promising higher returns on their investments. A lot of people can help you make money, but few people can help you ensure you know how to use your money to achieve your greatest goals in life. I need to know what makes my clients get up in the morning if I'm going to be of real use to them. Yes, I want to help their net worth grow, but I want that growth to help them fund the life they most want to live.

From the very first meeting, I make sure I convey to new clients how important it is for me to gain a true understanding of their situation. I ask follow-up questions, I rephrase questions, and sometimes I ask the same question twice so that I can get the fullest, most complete explanation. If clients say they want financial security, I'll ask them why. They might say they want to have enough money to last the rest of their lives. OK, why is that important? They might say, "Well, I have a son with mental illness to support, too." Suddenly, I've hit on an extremely important piece of information that gets to the heart of their valued relationships and goals. I needed that to come up with a meaningful plan.

If you're going through this process on your own without a financial planner, then I recommend questioning yourself and writing down your answers. Keep drilling down by asking "why?" until you reach the core values and aspirations behind your goals. If you want a bigger house, that's great—but spend the time to also figure out how that house fits into the overall meaning you're seeking in your life.

## GENERATING AN APPROPRIATE INVESTMENT PLAN

Using what we've learned in the discovery process, my team and I generate an individualized investment plan to position the client so that, in our opinion, they have the highest likelihood of achieving all that's important to them. We start with the investment plan because for nearly everyone, especially the more affluent, the number-one concern they have is making good decisions with their money. We meet with our client to review the investment plan and discuss why we think this is the best solution for them and their situation.

At the end of the investment plan meeting, we take a critical step that we've found is very unique in the investment advisory world. We ask the client to go home and reflect on the investment plan and review it on their own time. We suggest that they have somebody else look it over—someone whose opinion they trust in these matters. A week later, we'll get together again, answer any final questions or concerns they might have, and, in most cases, proceed with the original investment plan. Why do we do this? We want our clients to be as comfortable as they can be going forward, confident that this is indeed the best solution for them.

## THE ADVANCED PLAN

Once we have the fundamental investing advice squared away, it's time to focus on the Advanced Plan. We start this process with our own professional network team of experts we've assembled, each a highly qualified expert in their own field. In addition to myself, the team consists of a tax professional to help us focus on wealth enhancement concepts, a private client lawyer to help us with wealth transfer strategies, and an insurance professional who adds insight to the wealth protection part of the plan. On occasion, we'll round out the team with another professional from another field that may be pertinent to a particular client's situation.

The team meets, on our own time and away from the client, to review the client's situation. We discuss potential strategies to help that client in each of the four advanced-planning areas, and we brainstorm planning ideas that need to be on that particular client's radar. We develop raw strategies that we can later refine and develop as necessary to help that client achieve what's most important to them. Having a child with mental illness in the picture hugely affects the relevant planning areas for a client, so my team of professionals is well versed in issues of special needs.

Meeting with the team allows me to move the client into the advanced-planning phase I described above. By talking through their situation with a group of specialists—legal, tax, and insurance—I'm able to give more comprehensive advice about next steps. We each bring our own lens, and when we work together, we ensure we uncover all the important issues. Then, I can help the client navigate.

## REGULAR PROGRESS MEETINGS

Lives change. Goals change. Financial plans adapt. Because of this change, we like to meet with each client every six to twelve months to review the progress we've made so far and focus on the next item in our advanced planning. We review how the investment plan is working toward the client's goals and what, if anything, has changed in the client's life. The exact frequency we meet will depend on each client's situation. Just as you go to the doctor more frequently when you're treating an illness, it's helpful to meet with a wealth manager more frequently when you're getting your financial plan in order. If the client has a lot of unresolved items, such as needing to create an estate plan and set up financial instruments for a child with special needs, then we might agree to meet more frequently still. For someone who has a more stable situation, meeting annually is probably fine. It depends on the individual client's needs.

## FIRM GUIDANCE

As I discovered in my survey, many people dealing with mental illness in their families want a financial advisor to provide almost parental guidance. My business, Northstar Financial Planners, offers that kind of firm guidance if clients want it. If you're embarking on this process on your own, then you'll want to think about how you can hold yourself accountable and keep yourself on track without the external guidance and motivation of an empathetic advisor. How can you be a good parent to yourself on this topic?

If you decide to enlist a professional, then I encourage you to use the process outlined in this chapter as a template to make decisions about your advisor. Interview potential advisors about their approach. Will you always need to be the one to reach out to them, or will they follow up with you? If so, how often? What kinds of questions would they want to know about you as a new client?

Your advisor should want to know as much as you're willing to tell them, with the aim of getting to the heart of your goals and helping you achieve them. Ideally, once you choose an advisor, that relationship will last you for life, so it's worth taking extra time to ensure the fit is good at the beginning. An advisor worth keeping won't offer only a surface-level, transactional service; they will want to go deep.

## GUIDING QUESTIONS TO THINK ABOUT WHEN CREATING A COMPREHENSIVE FINANCIAL PLAN

1. What does your money mean to you?

2. What are your values with regard to money?

3. What do you want to achieve with your money (i.e., what are your goals)?

4. What assets do you have now? What debts?

5. What do you enjoy doing? What are your interests? These questions help uncover the underlying passions that your money can serve, allowing you to pursue the best version of your life.

6. Which relationships are most important to you? Consider family, community, neighbors, church members, work colleagues, and even pets. Some people bequeath assets to people who are not blood relations, so this question matters. Look for people who were important at one time but are no longer in the picture, such as estranged family members or ex-spouses. Sometimes, people don't realize their ex is still listed as a beneficiary on life insurance, for example, which means the ex (rather than the current spouse) would receive assets in the event of your death.

7. Who's giving you advice? For instance, who is your CPA? Who is your attorney, financial advisor, and insurance agent? For each, do you like this person? Are they doing a good job for you? Is the relationship a good one? Are they able to handle the complexity of your current life well?

8. Do you want or need to work with a professional financial advisor? If so, what kind of process do you want to follow with regard to planning and following up? How often do you see yourself meeting? What are your expectations of your advisor? (If you are your own advisor, what are your expectations of yourself?) Do you want your advisor to notify you if there's a drastic change in the stock market, for example? If you're developing and implementing a plan on your own, I encourage you to create a schedule for periodically revisiting your plan. Then think about what you'll do in various circumstances that might come up.

# CHAPTER FIVE

———

# Invest Efficiently

As parents of adult children coping with mental illness, you face the real possibility that your money must last not just your lifetime but your child's as well. That makes judicious investing critical to the success of your financial plan. Every other strategy I discuss in future chapters is designed to work in concert with investing. Start here.

How you invest matters. As your investment horizon is now two lifetimes, you have less room for the error, inefficiency, and waste that can be so common in investing. Every dollar has to go further, and every investment decision has to be made in the context of an investment plan that prioritizes efficiency and effectiveness. My goal for this chapter is for you to come away with efficient, evidence-based strategies for investing to make your money go further.

The strategies I discuss in this chapter apply regardless of the total value of your assets. Even if you only have a little bit of money, you can set some aside and allow it to grow over the long term; doing so is worthwhile. If you have more, even better. It all adds up. The effect of long-term compounding can really be staggering. If you'd had the ability to allocate one dollar across the breadth of the US large-cap stock markets in 1926, it would be worth over $5,000 today. That's a lot of growth for a single dollar.

I'll add that I'm not just handing out this advice to strangers—I give it to my own daughter. I recently persuaded her to set up an IRA and move $50 per month into an account. When she has enough to make the minimum purchase in a very low-cost mutual fund, that's what we invest in. Saving and investing $600 a year doesn't reap huge tax benefits for her right now, but it establishes a positive habit early on that will serve her well, and it provides the beginning of a nest egg for her over the long term. As you think about how to provide for your own child, consider how evidence-based investment strategies can provide a key part of your overall plan for success.

We'll discuss sound investment strategies later in the chapter, but in order to help you identify good investment choices from bad ones, I'll start with a negative object lesson: annuities. Because they are so often laden with comparably high fees, annuities are typically some of the most inefficient financial products you can choose, and as such, I'd argue, not a great fit for the needs of a parent of a child with severe mental illness. So what is an annuity?

## THE LURE OF ANNUITIES

An annuity, on its most basic level, is a promise from an entity that if you pay a lump sum, they will provide you a monthly income until your death, a guaranteed pension you can't outlive. Insurance companies have dreamed up many ways to make money in the annuity sector, so the products come in myriad forms. As a financial planner, I find myself getting cynical because I've seen so many annuity products that make a ton of money for the insurer without doing much to serve the purchaser.

Insurance companies make a lot of nice-sounding marketing promises that appeal to customers who seek security, who feel skittish about the market, and who don't have a good understanding of how capital markets work. A product that guarantees you won't lose money and offers a 3 percent annual return might sound great if you've just lost 10 percent in the stock market over the past year. However, 3 percent is well below the historical average return of a well-diversified market-based portfolio over the long term. Locking yourself into an annuity at that rate might feel comforting, but it most likely won't serve you well, in comparison to the other investment choices you could be making.

It's important to remember most insurance companies are for-profit businesses. They may very well promise you a guaranteed income for life and a guaranteed market upside without any downside, but they still have to make money on the transaction. Insurance companies are experts at understanding mortality tables and figuring out exactly how much they need to charge you given your age to come out ahead. While in very particular cases annuities can be helpful, when I've looked at my clients' annuities over many, many years, nearly all are so high-cost as to be ineffective.

## UNTANGLING AN ANNUITY MESS

A client I'll call Kristen came to me having bought a set of annuities, very proud of her purchases. I went through their details and felt like I needed to wash my hands afterward. They were laden with high fees and confusing contract language that I was pretty sure Kristen hadn't read. Annuities tend to be very expensive and complex products, and these were particularly bad.

As Kristen enthusiastically explained her reasoning for purchasing what she thought were wonderful products, I could tell she was not only recounting her insurance agent's sales pitch but also embellishing on it. Sales tactics elicit strange reactions in people: once we're hooked, we tend to magnify all the positive traits we hear and ignore any downsides. A salesperson might not even intentionally overpromise, but an excited customer still may come away from an interaction with unreasonably high expectations of a product's performance. Kristen's enthusiasm wasn't tempered by an understanding of the trade-offs involved in her purchases. She didn't have a realistic grasp of the benefits of these vehicles, and she certainly didn't know what alternative choices she was giving up.

In my field, we encounter situations like Kristen's all the time. People feel very confident and excited when they first purchase annuities. A few years down the road, they come to us scratching their heads. Something isn't adding up. They thought the value of the annuity would be worth more by now. When we model annuities' chances of achieving financial success on a variety of measures, they often perform very poorly. People cling to the guaranteed returns and the lack of exposure to market risk. But they forget or ignore what is often a bigger risk: inflation and the year-by-year erosion to their purchasing power.

Tax issues represent another fundamental problem with annuities. Insurance salespeople emphasize that as money grows in an annuity, it's not taxed. You're not paying capital gains or income taxes on the earnings. But there's a flipside: once you take money out of an annuity, any gains are taxed as ordinary income at the higher income rate, not the capital gains rate. You're deferring taxes but not avoiding them.

Once people start realizing annuities aren't serving them well, they face another financial hit in the form of likely surrender fees. Salespeople don't spend much time explaining that, if you want to back out of the contract down the road, you might have to sacrifice a surrender charge that could be as high as 10 percent of the money you've paid. The fees usually go down a little bit each year, incentivizing you to stay in the contract even if it's not working for you. Maybe the penalty starts at 10 percent, drops to 9 the next year, 8 the following year, and so on. You're facing years of backend surrender charges if you want out of the situation. Read the prospectus carefully, and you'll see in black and white exactly what the surrender charges are for the contract.

When we're untangling an annuity mess for a client like Kristen, we have to analyze the specifics of the situation and each annuity contract in order to make the best financial choices. We look at the annuity's current rate of return and the level of annual expenses in the contract, make a conservative estimate of the return the client could be making in other investments, and calculate the annuity's surrender fees now and for each year going forward. Depending on the fees and the potential gains from other investment vehicles, it could make sense to end an annuity contract today, even if it requires the payment of a surrender fee. We may find it's more advantageous to end the contract at some point in the future—perhaps two or three years from now. In most cases, once clients understand that even after they've paid the penalty they could be making more money elsewhere, they choose to follow our advice regarding when to make the switch.

In some cases, it makes sense to keep the money in an annuity for tax reasons—to avoid realizing any gains and having to pay tax on those gains. If our client is in a high-cost contract, we'll seek a lower-cost contract from a different insurer. We look for one with no commissions or surrender charges. A typical broker isn't going to recommend a no-commission product, because they don't make the broker money. By contrast, because we're in the comprehensive-planning business rather than a sales-centered business, we can recommend these lower-cost products, which we believe serve our clients' best interests. If it makes sense to choose a different annuity rather than pulling out of annuities entirely, then we can do what's called a 1035 exchange. Such an exchange is similar to an IRA rollover, and it allows us to get our clients into higher-quality, lower-cost annuities without having to realize any taxable gains.

As I mentioned earlier, one of the risks annuities are not very good at covering is inflation. Basically, everything you buy this year is going to cost you more next year, and keeping up with that increased amount is critical to maintaining purchasing power. Annuities, and especially fixed annuities with a fixed rate of return, have historically had a very difficult time keeping up with inflation. However, depending on a client's individual situation, goals, and risk tolerance, it often makes more sense to take on more market exposure in order to earn higher returns. This increase in market exposure can be perceived as "higher risk," a risk that typically doesn't refer to permanent loss so much as higher volatility. Over time, the markets have proven to offer so much more than a typical fixed-rate annuity could.

It's true that while there will be periods where the value goes up sharply, there will also be periods when the value of your investment goes down or stays stagnant. As long as you remain patient and disciplined, and you don't get skittish and sell off when the market is down, the down periods are simply fluctuations, not losses. Historically, investing in the market itself over the long term would have given you a much higher rate of return than what you would have earned in a fixed-rate product, and would have given you returns higher than the rate of inflation, so you would have maintained or increased your purchasing power.

Risk, return, and volatility are fundamental investing principles essential to consider when developing a successful financial plan. If they feel intimidating or confusing to you, you're not alone. I talk to extremely intelligent, accomplished, well-educated people who are terrified of the markets or think all market-based investments are Ponzi schemes. Given my professional experience and background, I can tell you that they are *not*, in fact, all scams. The way they work makes perfect sense to me. That understanding is part of the value I can offer my clients, and you may find value in consulting with a knowledgeable advisor, too.

In Kristen's case, it made sense to get her out of the annuities she'd purchased over a two-year period. As of this writing, we're in the process of helping her make that transition. We've eliminated the most egregious aspects of her situation without incurring tax penalties, and she's positioned now for better long-term returns. Equally important, she now understands the negative impacts commissions, fees, and penalties can have on her long-term investment goals. She sees why she needs to evaluate products with a clear head and not get swept up by slick sales presentations at fancy restaurant dinners paid for by salespeople. She can now focus on the most important aspect of an investment plan: balancing risk with the net return.

## WHAT PARENTS NEED TO UNDERSTAND ABOUT INVESTING EFFICIENTLY

I tell the story of untangling annuity messes because they're the opposite of investing efficiently. In my opinion, annuities are easily one of the least efficient investment vehicles for two reasons: fees and failure to make the best use of global capital markets. To understand investment efficiency, think about investing like a downhill skiing race. One skier, the efficient investment, points straight down the hill, takes the tightest lines, and goes as fast as possible. The other skier, the inefficient investment (such as an annuity), has to drag a big ball and chain. That second skier might figure out ways to go forward, but they'll be weighed down, slowed by the drag of the ball, and not performing well. They're definitely not going to cross the finish line first. The efficient, unencumbered skier is going to win.

In the skiing analogy, the ball and chain are the commissions, fees, and penalties. Investors have the same access to global capital markets, just as the skiers have access to the same ski slope. There's no such thing as a completely free investment, but there is a vast difference in the fees for investments. Let's say we're both invested in the stock market with different market-wide index funds, and the market we're investing in earns 10 percent one year. If I'm paying only half a percentage point toward fees in my fund and you're paying 2.5 percent, I'm going to net a

9.5 percent return while you're only going to net 7.5. I just won the race by quite a bit, even though we both had the same opportunities. In a stagnant year, when the markets gain nothing, that zero percent return would equate to my losing half a percent while you'd lose 2.5 percent. These differences compound year over year. I keep more each year in this scenario and, in turn, earn even more year over year than you do, even if we started with the same amount of money and invested in the same market.

No one wants to waste money or lose out on potential returns. In the case of a family having to provide lifetime support for a child with mental illness, you need your dollars to stretch as far as they possibly can. That means you need the costs associated with your investments to get as low as possible and the net returns as high as possible as a result. Even a fraction of a percent more in returns could make a huge difference in your child's life. Depending on the overall value of your portfolio, that fraction could, for example, fund a few more years of their expenses. From that perspective, minimizing fees is a life-and-death issue.

## THE TRADITIONAL APPROACH IS INEFFICIENT

I've found from personal experience that investment salespeople don't focus on efficiency. My firm manages more than $150 million in investments, so on occasion, companies marketing investment products offer to fly me to fancy sales conferences for a few days. These events consist of a few dozen vendors in a big hotel ballroom. All the companies want me to do is go around and hear their pitch, because they hope I'll then use their products in my clients' portfolios. The first question I ask each one is "What are your fees?" It's shocking how few of them know the answer off the top of their head. Fine, then, I'll ask to see their prospectus, since the fees are listed there.

All the vendors want to talk about is "sizzle," which unfortunately is what a lot of advisors want to hear. They focus on how they're going to beat the market return, and they give other promises they rarely are able to deliver on over the long term. They want to talk about how smart they are, but honestly, as someone who knows better, I don't care what their salesperson says. If you ask me to evaluate a list of investment vehicles, I will always start by ranking them by cost. For the rest of the event, I'm polite to these salespeople, but I'm not going to recommend my clients use an unnecessarily expensive product, no matter how smart they claim to be or how exciting their new algorithm for beating the market is.

To return to the downhill-skiing race analogy, just as all racers are on the same slope, all investment funds within the same market interact with the same investment choices. There's a total return that market will deliver, and your chances of beating that by trying to guess which investments are better than other investments are very slim. For most people—as in nearly everybody—you are better off having a cross section of the market and not trying to pick out the "good investments." No matter how smart your people are, you're probably not going to beat the market any more than a skier is going to defy the laws of gravity or change the shape of the slope. If we're all on the same slope, let's bet on the skier who is the least weighed down—that is, let's pick the fund with the lowest costs.

Suppose you want to invest in a fund focusing on stocks of large companies in the United States. One fund simply invests evenly in the stocks of the one thousand largest companies in that sector. That's a straightforward, essentially automated strategy that charges a low fee as a result. Another fund also invests in large-company US stocks, but it's run by a highly credentialed investment manager whose company literature states he has a great track record of beating the market. The literature goes on to explain how he and his team research the companies in this sector and are able to pick only those companies that are the highest performers. He manages the fund actively by keeping tabs on the performance of each of its holdings throughout the year and buying what he thinks are the top one hundred to two hundred securities that will outperform the overall market. There are two main problems with his approach. First of all, it's going to cost more. Hopefully that's obvious. He'll have higher trading costs, more costs in analysis, and higher tax ramifications. In addition, he'll probably have more staff and human resource costs to pay. We know that actively traded investment funds as a group have higher costs than passive strategy funds. So not only does he have to outperform the market, but he has to do it by the difference in costs between his method and the other method of simply buying everything in the market. Second, I'd argue he's not really bringing anything to the table with his history of out-performance other than a lucky streak. Study after study points to the conclusion that the number of active managers that do beat an average market return is the same number that you would expect to beat the market simply by chance. They do exist, but identifying who they are going to be, who the "winning" managers are, ahead of the fact is the tricky part.

To make the most out of your assets, keep your costs low. You want your money to go toward your highest priorities—including supporting your child with mental illness—and not toward the bank account of a Wall Street stock picker.

## MY EXPERIENCE ON THE DARK SIDE

I started my career on what I have come to think of as the financial dark side, meaning the side focused on sales. When I started my career in 1991, all I knew was that financial advising was all about selling products to make money, and advisors sold what their employer wanted them to sell. Not at all coincidentally, those were the products that would make the employers the most money: the least efficient products the customer could buy—the higher costs hurt the customers' returns, but the fees went right into the company's pocket. At the time, I didn't realize alternative models existed. Today, my path to fee-only, fiduciary-level advising has fortunately become more common in the industry, though there are still a lot of sales-focused advisors out there earning commissions from the sale of products.

I know firsthand that if you do seek professional financial advice, it's important to consider the source. The way we've learned how markets actually work from the academic world is different from the way they're so often portrayed by Wall Street. Financial advisors who are focused on selling you products will not paint a complete picture of how you can invest with the most efficient strategies as a consumer. There are more choices out there than what they're showing you—choices that do not give them commissions or pay them directly.

When I was on the traditional sales side of the business, I wanted to gain a deeper understanding of how markets work. I read academic white papers from some of the best minds in the fields of finance and economics. At first, I found myself arguing with their points. They were saying that active management had some serious flaws, which was the opposite of what I'd learned. My first impulse was that they were wrong. Then I realized they didn't have an incentive to spread misinformation. Their goal was simply to describe how markets work, and many of them had won Nobel Prizes or other recognition for their findings. Over time, it became clear what I'd learned about investing from the traditional financial sales model was more about how to sell those investments and not really about how to invest efficiently.

I found myself in a difficult spot conflicted between two goals—helping people achieve all that's important to them in the most efficient manner I knew, and making a living. I had come to the realization that the products I was selling and earning commissions on weren't the best possible choices for my clients, and I knew it. I loved my work, but to continue, I had to change the method of how I got paid. It couldn't be based on product sales. It had to be based on truly serving the needs of the clients. What if a client didn't need an annuity, life insurance policy, mutual fund, or some other investment? What if all they needed was sound advice that had no product recommendation? I needed to be able to provide that advice, and to be able to make a living doing it. From that start, I went on to found my current firm, Northstar Financial Planners.

At first, I thought I could make money by charging flat fees to write financial plans for people. In 2000, though, clients didn't want me to write long plans for them. The tech bubble was bursting. Clients wanted help understanding what was going on with their portfolios. Because I was continuing to read academic investment theory, I started counseling my clients based on what I'd learned. Instead of doling out the typical Wall Street advice of picking the hot fund or the next Microsoft, I suggested they diversify in global capital markets, periodically rebalance, and reduce their costs to the lowest levels possible. I couldn't promise them my plan would completely rectify the state of their portfolio in the short term, as the US markets were in a down phase. However, based on my understanding of underlying market principles, my strategy offered a sound direction for long-term growth and was more in line with their true long-term goals.

I talked my clients through my reasoning, and the ones who followed my advice were happy with the results. Three years down the road, we were able to compare what they would have earned staying in their original US-focused, high-fee portfolios versus what they achieved with a diversified, lower-cost strategy. The benefits of global diversification were obvious. I had started by looking at historical comparisons and having faith in the theories I'd read. As it turned out, the principles I uncovered in the academic literature, known as modern portfolio theory (MPT), led to highly effective practices. My results shouldn't be surprising, because academics just want to know what works best; they aren't incentivized to sell particular products. But the academic strategies, despite their efficacy, just aren't at all common in the financial world—because they don't earn high commissions.

## PRINCIPLES COME FIRST

I follow a set of investment principles that is based in academic financial theory and history, and it has several elements. Having a comfort level with your investments and peace of mind is about more than simply returns. It starts with a firm set of principles that form good practices. The first principle is **rational optimism**, what I sometimes call faith because it operates out of the gut as much as the reason. Rational optimism is the result of looking at all we know that has happened in the past and what that means for how we think about the future. When we look at the curve of human progress, what we see is quite stunning. Advances in technology, medicine, and virtually every aspect of human growth continue to accelerate at mind-boggling rates.

Markets reflect this curve of human progress. When markets drop, that drop can only be temporary, as the curve of human progress continues to surge forward and upward. Markets have no choice but to catch back up with that progress. You want to be there when they do. Rational optimism about the future comes from looking at the history of the market, seeing regular market drops, recognizing that they occur somewhat frequently, and realizing there's nothing to suggest the market won't always rebound. The drops—and the recoveries—are normal. Just since World War II, there have been more than a dozen of these corrections, including the 2001 tech bubble burst and the 2008 Great Recession, sometimes amounting to a sudden decrease in value of 30 or even 50 percent in the US market. Yes, that's a lot. It feels like financial Armageddon. The news media have a field day talking about the end of the financial world. Yet if we look at the data, the value always comes back.

Rational optimism believes that markets will rebound. This is what informs my advice to clients like Kristen who worry about volatility. A drop in the market isn't a loss, as long as you hold on to your position and wait for the value to come back, rather than panicking and selling. Because we believe the markets will continue to work the way they've always worked, we'll stick to the long-term strategy and not get rattled by volatility—even extreme volatility.

In addition to having a rationally optimistic view of the future, we need steadfast **patience**. This is the second principle you must embrace to have a favorable investment experience. We live in an impatient, frantic society. When there is a market correction, the media shrieks we should do something! Get out of the market, get into a different sector of the market, buy, sell, try this latest fix—just *do something*. Traditional advice gives the impression we can control what happens in capital markets, but we can't. Let them fluctuate. Keep following your strategy, ride out the dip, and be patient. You may feel like you're overriding your natural instinct and running into a burning building instead of out of it. But if you have an evidence-based strategy and stick to it instead of reacting frantically, you can be rationally optimistic that you'll be fine in the end.

In addition to patience, we require **discipline**. Having discipline means you continue doing what you know is right, based on evidence and a preset strategy. You're not swayed by the not-so-gentle urgings of the financial press during a financial crisis or even a minimal market downturn. You stay the course and continue forward, ignoring those exiting in fear. Your fearful side might urge you to sell off and avoid exposure to any more risk. You need to listen to your rational, intellectual side instead. Instead of selling in the down market, it's time to buy. Prices are low—everything is on sale. It's like going into your favorite store and finding everything you want is 50 percent off, and there aren't even any lines. In the 2008–2009 downturn, I asked my clients, "When will you possibly see a better time to buy again in your lifetime?" Buying low means realizing maximum gains when the market rebounds, which we believe it will because we have a rationally optimistic view of the future (and we've never been wrong so far—as long as the market has existed, it's always rebounded). People who purchased during the downturn, and who waited out the correction, were rewarded for having that discipline.

## PARENTS CANNOT AFFORD TO HAVE INEFFICIENT PORTFOLIOS

If you're reading this book, you're concerned about financial planning so that you can give your child with mental illness the best life possible. Keep that priority at the forefront, and let it guide your decisions about costs. Every penny wasted on excess inefficiency is a penny that could have gone to supporting your son or daughter. The more you save in fees, the more you can benefit from compound interest over time. Reduce your investment costs to the lowest level you can.

### DON'T BE TOO CONSERVATIVE

Inflation is a fact of financial life—ignore it at your peril. Depending on the state of the economy, inflation in a given year might run anywhere from 2 to 5 percent or more. In my lifetime, I've seen inflation run into the double digits. That means that most everything you bought this year is going to cost more next year and every year after. If you don't earn at least as much interest as the rate of inflation, your assets lose purchasing power over time. People who don't understand the impact of inflation stick to less volatile, lower-yield investments or even cash. In their attempt to avoid losing money to volatility, they lose money to inflation. The higher volatility of global capital markets comes with higher returns. You need those higher returns to outpace inflation and make the most of your money. Whether you have a lot of money or a little, investing is an important piece of a solid financial plan to support yourself and your child over two lifetimes. Don't neglect it!

The key to striking a balance between risk and return is to take smart, evidence-based risks. Go with the risk that has historically paid off over the long term. History and theory both point toward a diversified global portfolio of stocks and bonds as the smart risk.

Good financial planners help make sound, evidence-based decisions about the kinds of investments to choose and how to allocate your money within those investment classes. They have the expertise to cut through the noise of salespeople, Wall Street, and the media and get you on a path that will actually work. They'll help you stick to your strategy when you get scared; they'll remind you why it's not a good idea to sell low and cling to a lot of cash. In our firm, when the markets take a dive, we return to the mantra of rational optimism, patience, and discipline. We help our clients keep their priorities and the evidence in the forefront instead of whatever reactionary financial information they're hearing from acquaintances or the news.

Planning to have enough money to last your entire life and your dependent child's entire life is a game of patience. If you're a young couple saving to buy a house on a certain date, market volatility over the short term might make putting your down payment in the market too risky; you may or may not get the full amount out on that particular day. However, retirement and your child's future are decades-long processes, and historical evidence points to a diversified exposure to global markets as the strategy that will serve you best. If you're only drawing 3 to 5 percent of your assets each year, then your portfolio will have a chance to grow during the bull markets and rebound from the bear markets.

## GOOD INVESTMENT PLANS ARE SURPRISINGLY SIMPLE

It is much simpler to create an effective investment plan than most people realize. Wall Street wants you to believe you have to have extensive expertise in fundamental analysis, investigating the characteristics of particular companies, learning them inside and out, and choosing which ones will win based on their future plans and how they're responding to competitors. In reality, stock picking isn't effective. It's more important to know how asset classes work together than what individual stocks within an asset class are doing.

Asset classes are groups of stocks or bonds that behave similarly. Such classes include US stocks, large company stocks, international small companies, or long-term corporate bonds, just to name a few. Stocks and bonds within a given class tend to move together in the same direction. Even if one company is doing better than another at any particular time, for the most part, all the participants in the same class generally move up or down at the same time. You can think of stocks in a given class like a flock of starlings. When one turns left, they all turn left, even though some are closer to or farther from the ground. Another class might be a flock of geese. The geese all move together, but they have nothing to do with the starlings. When the starlings fly off, the geese might fly in the same direction, a different direction, or be hunkered down in the grass. The movement of one has little to do with the other, just like US stocks tend to move independently of stocks in other countries' markets.

Academics study asset classes and identify the characteristics of the separate groups and how they are correlated, or related, to one another. To use the bird analogy, the degree of correlation tells us whether the geese are always in the grass when the starlings are in the air, whether they always go left when the starlings go left, or whether there's no relationship between the two groups' actions. For the purposes of this discussion, though, the important point is that your advisor—or you, if you're planning to manage your investments on your own—will need an understanding of the different classes out there so you can diversify and distribute your risk.

The excellent news is you don't need a stock-picking guru. If you were to track the performance of the different asset classes and then graph their performance over fifteen years, I guarantee you would not find a clear pattern in their fluctuations. Each class is up sometimes and down sometimes, but these times are random. The only overall pattern is that, despite the volatility, all the classes have an upward trend over the long term.

Once people realize that there isn't a pattern anyone can identify in order to play the market perfectly, they have an aha moment: Why not just allocate money across the available classes? That way, your money will increase in value over time, and you won't have to worry about which asset class happens to do the best in a given period. Diversification also helps balance out your portfolio's overall volatility: because asset classes move independently of each other, when one is down, another is usually up.

Some investors mistakenly think diversification simply means owning a lot of different stocks, but that's not accurate. If you own three hundred stocks and they're all starlings, then they'll all go up or down at the same time. Your overall portfolio will do well when the starling class is doing well and badly when the starling class tanks. True diversification means having some starlings but also some geese, eagles, peacocks, and other species moving independently of each other. If you have a foundational understanding of how markets work, then the answer to successful investing becomes almost self-evident: diversify, spread the risk, keep costs low, and maintain a long view.

## ALIGN INVESTMENT MANAGEMENT WITH YOUR FINANCIAL GOALS

Good investment advisors determine your goals and then manage your portfolio accordingly. If you want to buy a second house or take a big vacation, part of your portfolio should be designated for that purpose. If you lie awake at night worrying you or your child with special needs might reach a point where the account balance is zero, then your advisor should be focusing on long-term wealth enhancement and protection instead. The exact formula and direction of your strategy has to unfold from your goals.

## PRACTICAL GUIDANCE FOR YOUR INVESTMENT PLAN

If you take away any advice from this chapter, I hope it's the emphasis on asset allocation, and the importance of getting your costs as low as possible. Academic research backs up my focus on diversifying your portfolio across stock and bond asset classes as opposed to a strategy concentrated on picking good stocks over bad stocks and market timing. A diverse portfolio of investments with the lowest costs possible is the best approach.

How do you compare costs? Fortunately, the costs of various investment fund options are publicly available. Morningstar.com offers a user-friendly research option for the average consumer. If you know the symbol for a given mutual fund or exchange-traded fund (ETF), you can search for it on Morningstar and find the cost both expressed as a percentage and rated in comparison to other funds of that type. (In other words, a particular fund might have "very high," "average," or "low" costs compared to its competitors with similar fund types.) Shop around and find a fund with a low percentage for its type.

## REASON FOR HOPE

I've covered a lot of nitty-gritty investing information, but my overarching message is that there's hope for your financial success. We have every reason to be rationally optimistic the markets will serve us well over the long term. The markets come with volatility; while we can temper the worst of it with the right allocation mix for you, you should still expect ups and downs. If we stay the course, however, we have every reason to believe the markets will bring us good returns over the long term—as they always have in the past. With rational optimism, patience, and discipline, investing in a diverse array of stocks and bonds allows us to outpace inflation, increase our purchasing power, expand our wealth, support ourselves, and maximize our children's quality of life. Coming to the investing process with a basic understanding of risk, costs, and net returns greatly improves your likelihood of positive financial results. Monetary returns will then increase your chances of meeting your most valued goals.

# CHAPTER SIX

—

# ABLE Accounts

My wife has a savings account in her name that we think of as our son's money. We plan the ultimate use of the funds to be for his benefit, but we can't put them in his name, because doing so would eliminate his eligibility for government benefits. The informal arrangement makes sense for us at this moment, but by itself, it's not sufficient for our son to supplement his benefits for things like housing and transportation, not to mention the healthcare not covered by Medicaid he will need over the course of his lifetime. That's where an ABLE account can make a difference.

In 2014, Congress wanted to help people with disabilities have funds to live above the subsistence level without losing their benefits. So, that year it amended the tax code to allow people with disabilities to have tax-advantaged cash assets in their name in what's called an Achieving a Better Life Experience (ABLE) account. At the time of this writing, such accounts can be opened in thirty-seven states plus the District of Columbia. The list of participating states continues to grow.

ABLE accounts are fantastic financial-planning tools for families who have children with special needs. As I was helping a client set one up for her child, it hit me: I didn't yet have one set up for my own son. Sometimes, I'm like the shoeless cobbler—I'm so focused on helping my clients I forget to tend to my own situation. If you're just now hearing about ABLE accounts or have put off setting one up, don't feel bad. As funny as it sounds, I've been there!

## HOW ABLE ACCOUNTS FIT INTO A SYSTEMATIC FINANCIAL PLAN

An ABLE account won't solve all your financial challenges, but it's a planning tool that will complement other aspects of your plan. One of the biggest mistakes families make is inadvertently eliminating their child's eligibility for government benefits. Once the child has more than $2,000 in countable cash assets—whether because of a big birthday check, an inheritance, or simply failing to spend enough in a given month—the benefits go away. An ABLE account offers a great way to handle gifts and other potential income streams while continuing to benefit from

SSI or SSDI, Supplemental Nutrition Assistance Program (SNAP), and Medicaid. It's a powerful financial tool that complements both applying for government benefits and establishing a special needs trust, which I'll discuss in the next chapter. As such, in most cases (including mine), it makes sense to take advantage of the ABLE legislation for your situation.

You can put up to $15,000 per year into an ABLE account, have a balance in the account of up to $100,000, and still retain eligibility for SSI, SSDI, and Medicaid. The ABLE account is in your child's name, giving them control of funds, which they can access now or at any point in the future. Your child can spend the ABLE money on anything that enhances their quality of life, health, or independence. Eligible expenses include education, housing, transportation, employment training and support, assistive technologies, personal support services, healthcare expenses, and financial management and administrative services. The primary restriction on using the funds is that they can't be given away as a gift to people other than the beneficiary.

ABLE accounts draw from the structure of 529 college savings plans. They're investment accounts rather than cash, and their growth is tax-free. States underwrite both ABLE accounts and 529 plans. Each state chooses which mutual funds it will offer through its plans. Once you establish an account, you can look at the offerings and choose the portfolio option that maximizes diversification while minimizing cost—the same principles from our investment discussion apply just as much to an ABLE account as to a set of stocks. You'll want the lowest fees and the most diversity of asset classes. As such, it's important to research the plans offered within a given state's account. They vary from state to state, and some are more expensive. Some, but not all, states offer reciprocal investing; for example, as of this writing, people in Florida can invest in Tennessee's plans but not vice versa. So, if your state doesn't offer an ABLE account directly, do your research, as another state's account may be available to you.

I'd recommend research for everyone, in fact, so that you can make the best choice for your situation. The ABLE National Resource Center website, ABLENRC.org, is a great place to start reviewing your options. The website allows you to build a spreadsheet comparing and contrasting the plans offered by up to three states so that you can review costs and make an informed decision. As we've talked about, the principles of good investing apply as much to ABLE accounts as to your overall portfolio. States aren't trying to make a profit off these plans, so it's possible to find funds with comparable costs to your personal investments. Look for them.

Why choose an ABLE account rather than a special needs

trust (covered in the next chapter)? An ABLE account gives your child a way to save up to $100,000, using a vehicle that costs less and offers more flexibility than a trust. The individual with special needs can access the funds in their ABLE account directly, rather than having to ask a trustee. They simply fill out a form specifying how much money they need and its purpose—for example, $X$ amount of money to buy a car. They submit that form to the ABLE plan and get a check in return. Then they'll be able to use the money to pay the dealership directly. Because of the provisions of the ABLE legislation, this is the one case where having more than $2,000 in cash assets for a very brief period is acceptable without losing government benefits. Many state ABLE accounts also come with a debit card option, making smaller withdrawals easier than filling out a form.

You may have concerns about an ABLE account for your child suffering from a mental illness if that mental illness affects your child's cognitive ability. ABLE accounts were not conceived exclusively for those suffering from mental illness disabilities but rather for all disabilities. I want to make it clear that your child has full access to the account. Any monies paid out of the account are paid directly to your child, who then uses the money to pay for his/her chosen purchase. Short of having a full guardianship or a legal document proving your child has given up control of the account, there's very little you could do to prevent a withdrawal for any reason. It's your child's money. You may want to think about this before setting up an ABLE account if you feel your child's cognitive ability, when it comes to money, could be a concern.

## ABLE ACCOUNT STRUCTURE AND OFFERINGS

As I mentioned, ABLE accounts are built on a Section 529 savings plan chassis, meaning that you can technically contribute up to whatever a state's 529 maximum is (in the case of Florida, it's $350,000). However, an account balance higher than $100,000 ends the beneficiary's eligibility for Social Security income. At that point, rather than risking your child's government benefits, it's time to look at a special needs trust for additional funds. I'll discuss this option in more depth in the next chapter.

As of 2018, you can roll the balance of an existing 529 plan into an ABLE account. Such a rollover is a great option once your child receives a mental health diagnosis. They can still use the money for college if an educational track remains on the table, but they're able to access it for other needs as well. If your child is the beneficiary on a 529 account worth more than $100,000, you should roll over some of it into an ABLE account and then designate a new beneficiary for the rest. If you don't have a second child, you could change the beneficiary to a different blood relative; put the excess into a special needs trust, as we'll discuss in the next chapter; or roll over the entire amount and spend the excess immediately on something that will benefit your child under the ABLE rules, such as a car. However, by keeping the money in 529 and ABLE accounts, you maximize tax advantages, provide a fund for your child with special needs, and protect their Social Security eligibility, which is why I recommend that option when looking at 529 rollovers.

ABLE accounts are not a commissionable product, so sales-based financial advisors don't generally have an incentive to recommend them or set them up. I'd be somewhat surprised if they are even on their radar. If you're currently working with an advisor whose compensation is based on commissions, you may want to seek help from a fee-only advisor if you need help researching and setting up your child's ABLE account.

Helping people set up accounts where there are no commissions involved is an area where fee-only, fiduciary advisors excel. By definition, they are required to put your best financial interests over their own. When ABLE accounts first came out, my firm did all the research and legwork for our first client to use such an account. It was good for us to know what each state was offering and which had the best plans. We set up a spreadsheet of our findings, which we keep updated and have used to help him as well as subsequent parents of children with special needs.

It's also possible to set up one of these accounts on your own if you do your due diligence, but it's work-intensive and may require a steep learning curve for someone new to financial planning. Professional financial advisors can be helpful, since they should have more familiarity with all the options, whereas the information is new to you.

### DETAILS TO KEEP IN MIND

In order to be eligible to open an ABLE account, your child must have received a disability diagnosis that meets Social Security criteria prior to their twenty-sixth birthday. Maybe you aren't getting around to opening the account until they're twenty-eight, but the diagnosis must already have been in place prior to age twenty-six.

ABLE eligibility is one more reason to apply for SSI or SSDI benefits regardless of your financial situation. If your child meets the age criteria and is also receiving benefits already from SSI or SSDI, they are automatically eligible to establish an ABLE account. If they're not a recipient of SSI or SSDI, but still meet the age of onset disability requirement, they could still be eligible to open an ABLE account if they meet the Social Security definition and criteria for disability and receive a letter of certification from a licensed physician. Your child does not have to be receiving Social Security disability benefits in order to meet the criteria for setting up an ABLE account. However, if your child is receiving Social Security and was diagnosed prior to age twenty-six, they're in. I reiterate: go apply for SSI or SSDI!

## DON'T OVERFUND

The yearly maximum contribution for an ABLE account is currently $15,000 total from all sources combined. If you personally put in $10,000 one year, then additional combined contributions from grandparents or other family members can't exceed $5,000 that year. The total amount in the account shouldn't be allowed to exceed $100,000, or the beneficiary will become ineligible for Social Security benefits.

## MEDICAID PAYBACK PROVISION

When the beneficiary of an ABLE account dies, the state has the right to file a claim to recoup the amount it spent on Medicaid for that beneficiary, up to the residual amount in the account. For that and other reasons, it doesn't make sense to hoard money in an ABLE account until death. The funds should be spent on an ongoing basis to support the beneficiary's quality of life.

## SUMMARY

ABLE accounts provide a great option for helping to supplement your child's benefits from SSI, SSDI, private insurance, and Medicaid, with lower costs and more flexibility than a special needs trust. For families with the ability to save more than $100,000 in assets, the account works very well in tandem with the special needs trust, to provide additional benefits and options for the family. A fiduciary wealth manager can be extremely helpful in navigating the ins and outs of using these accounts to the best advantage in the context of an overall financial plan.

# CHAPTER SEVEN

---

# Special Needs Trusts

It's very common for clients to tell me they have two children—one with special needs and one without—and they simply plan to leave all their money to the one without special needs and expect him or her to take care of the sibling. They know their children are good people and feel confident the healthy one will take care of the other.

I don't doubt the healthy child has good intentions, but a lot can go wrong with this plan. The money can easily be diverted along the way instead of benefitting the child with mental illness. For instance, what happens if the inheritor dies and doesn't have an estate plan leaving money to the sibling? If the inheritor's children want to pocket the money, there's nothing stopping them. What if the inheritor gets early onset dementia and stops making good decisions, or gets divorced and has to split assets with the former spouse? In each of those cases, the parents' money wouldn't get used to care for their child in the way they'd intended. Too many variables make relying on a healthy sibling to honor a verbal agreement a bad idea. Instead, I recommend taking legal steps to ensure your estate is used in accordance with your wishes.

At my firm, one of the things we focus on during the discovery phase of the financial-planning process is unpacking our clients' current estate plans and how they could be improved. For instance, if the client is planning on a healthy child caring for a sibling, does the healthy child know about, agree to, and understand that arrangement? By discussing potential issues, families often begin to see problems with their plan and start considering better approaches. They may also be under the mistaken impression that their will is sufficient to ensure their child's welfare, when, in fact, a large dollar amount of direct inheritance could actually have a negative impact. The mentally ill child may not be able to manage a large sum of money, and even if they could, the inheritance would wipe out their government benefits.

Special needs trusts prevent the problems listed above. They include provisions to maintain SSI or SSDI and Medicaid. They spell out exactly how the money should be used in service of maintaining the child's quality of life. They also protect the funds from being drained by creditors or legal judgments—if your child gets unlucky or makes a legal or financial mistake, you don't want their source of support to evaporate.

## ANY AMOUNT MAKES A DIFFERENCE

I'll discuss some big numbers in this chapter, but any amount you set aside in a trust will make a difference to your child's quality of life. A trust doesn't have to be huge to have a positive impact. It can supplement government benefits to improve your child's standard of living, in a big or even a small way. For instance, a trust distribution might ensure your child can buy lunch every day of the month, and that's a worthy, meaningful goal.

Keep in mind the trust you leave behind is also a gesture of caring for your child. Decades ago, my wife's grandmother set up a fund for her through the American Bible Society. My wife is now in her fifties, but every year, she still receives a check for about $50 from this fund. The amount is insignificant, but it's a lifetime gift from her grandmother. It's special.

## WHAT IS A SPECIAL NEEDS TRUST?

A special needs trust is a legal instrument allowing you to leave money for the care of a beneficiary, e.g., a child with mental illness. It is a big step toward building a good answer to the core question the interviewees in my study raised: What will happen to my child after I die? Special needs trusts provide for the needs of the recipient, and can only be established by a parent, grandparent, legal guardian, or court order. In other words, you can't set one up for your neighbor who doesn't seem to be receiving good care from their parents—that is, unless you go through the process of getting a court order allowing it.

I've seen resources online that suggest writing your own special needs trust, but I unequivocally discourage this practice. A trust is a legal instrument that must be worded, structured, and signed correctly in order to operate as you intend. For this reason, I strongly recommend working with a lawyer to create your trust, specifically one experienced with special needs trusts in particular. A lawyer experienced in this field will know the type of special needs trust to use and will include all the essential details to ensure your wishes are carried out accurately in a way that allows for continuing benefits for your child.

## CHOOSING A TRUSTEE

The special needs trust exists as a legal entity, so its provisions remain in force after you die. In the beginning, you would likely be the trustee of a trust you've created, though you don't have to be. When you reach an age or condition that no longer allows you to fulfill this role, the language of the trust will specify either your healthy child or another trustee takes over.

The buck stops with the trustee, as they're in charge of making decisions in the interest of the beneficiary—in this case, your child with mental illness. It's important for the trustee to be both responsible and well versed in the provisions of the trust—they have to know what they can and can't do with the money. What they can't do with the money is almost more important than what they can. Can they buy stock options with it? What about real estate? Can they buy any real estate with it, such as investment properties, or only a single house for the beneficiary to live in? If you want to limit or control the investment options, there has to be a paragraph in the document covering each of these situations and more.

Because there are so many situations to address, trust documents often run twenty to thirty pages or even longer. They can be as long as you need them to be in order to explain your desires for every situation you can think of. As long as what you're specifying is legal, you can include anything you want. For instance, you might include an age minimum for the beneficiary to start receiving funds— that age can be whatever you decide. The document is essentially the law book for the world of your particular trust, and the trustee enforces the law.

Choosing a good trustee is similar to choosing a good financial advisor: you're putting a tremendous amount of trust in this person, so choose carefully. If it's a family member, make sure they understand the responsibility they would be taking on. If you are considering a corporate trustee, research their experience. Meet with them. Ask them hard questions. Ask them as many questions as you can think of—there are no bad questions. You want to know as much as you possibly can about them and how they will approach looking out for the best financial interests of your child. Depending on your goals and the language of your specific trust, you could specify there should always be a corporate cotrustee to help advise on the best management of the funds. You might specify the healthy child who succeeds you as trustee could have the option of firing an ineffective corporate trustee and hiring someone else. These are specifics you'd want to discuss with your lawyer, but it's good to think through the different situations and dynamics you'd want your trust to address.

It's important to pick an honest and reliable trustee to follow the provisions of the trust and to have a plan in place in case the trustee dies or needs to step down. Ideally, you'd have a list of successor trustees in the event of death or inability to fulfill the role. The list would end with an ultimate trustee, which would most commonly be a corporate trustee experienced with managing trusts for people.

I would *not* recommend designating your financial advisor as the trustee, even if they work with you on a fiduciary basis and do a great job. My firm refuses to act as trustee for any of our clients, because we feel it's a conflict of interest. We don't think any entity should be vested with that much power—to recommend and help fund a trust, to direct the investment of its assets, *and* to make decisions about the funds' distribution. You want a trustee who will monitor the beneficiary's best interests, keep tabs on the people who are supposed to serve the beneficiary, and ensure everything remains aboveboard.

If the trust is for a person with mental illness, the trustee might have to evaluate some strange or inappropriate requests for money. The beneficiary's cognitive abilities are often compromised or in decline, so they might ask for things that are obviously outside the guidelines of the trust. I've heard of many parents fielding very odd requests for money for things that the adult children with mental illness clearly shouldn't have or do, and they have to say, "Sorry, no. I wish we could help you with that, but we can't."

Finally, in designating a trustee, you have to consider their knowledge not only of the trust document itself but also of important issues related to your child's care. Specifically, it's important for the trustee to understand Social Security and Medicaid. A major purpose of establishing a trust is so you can designate a large amount of money to be used for the welfare of your child without making them ineligible for government benefits. Whoever administers the trust needs to understand the ins and outs of maintaining this eligibility.

## TRUST TYPES AND REVOCABILITY

There are three main types of special needs trusts: the first-party trust, the third-party trust, and the pooled trust. All three types name the person with special needs as the beneficiary. First-party trusts are funded with assets that belong to the person with the disability or assets that the disabled person receives directly—for example, an inheritance, a gift, a court award, or an accident settlement. If the person wants to qualify for government benefits, they have to get their cash assets under $2,000 before they can receive any benefits. They create a trust and move all their assets into it so that they now meet the eligibility requirements for SSDI and Medicaid. The trust has a Medicaid payback provision just like the one we discussed for ABLE accounts. Medicaid essentially agrees to allow the beneficiary to have access to more than $2,000 in their own assets as long as it can be reimbursed by funds left in the trust when the beneficiary dies. The decision of the beneficiary to transfer their assets into the first-party trust is irrevocable—they can't change their mind and move their funds back into their name. It's a tremendously consequential choice to make. In this case, it's a prudent one: the beneficiary is permanently disabled, and qualifying for government benefits will help ensure their long-term quality of life.

Parents have the option of setting up third-party trusts, which are funded by someone other than the beneficiary, but also irrevocable. It's a stand-alone trust that can receive property from your will, living trust, life insurance policy, your IRA, or basically any asset from people other than the disabled person who want to help the person with special needs. I have one set up for my son as a way for relatives to give gifts that will benefit him without jeopardizing his Social Security and Medicaid eligibility. A key benefit of the third-party trust is that it is not subject to the Medicaid payback provision that is in the first-party trust. This means that when the beneficiary dies, the remaining assets in the trust can go to other family members, or to a charity, rather than back to the government. It makes sense to keep those gifts separate from a first-party trust in order to prevent them from being subject to the Medicaid payback provision.

A pooled trust is an alternative to the first-party special needs trust, which we'll discuss in a moment.

The examples I've given illustrate why it might make sense to have multiple special needs trusts. In affluent families, children may already have a significant amount of assets in their name before becoming legally disabled. Those assets would go in a first-party trust. The parents then may want to put part of their assets into a third-party trust to benefit the child after they're gone, without the inheritance having a negative impact on government benefits. There are different legal instruments you can set up to fulfill distinct but related purposes to benefit your child, and as such, it's useful to talk with a lawyer experienced in this field to help you navigate the complex decisions you'll need to make.

## CARING FOR THE BENEFICIARY WHILE MAINTAINING FAMILY RELATIONSHIPS

A key benefit of the trust is to pay for the things your child with mental illness needs. Since you're creating the trust, you can use its language to define what those things are, along with the required language your attorney will use. Your child will make requests for funds to buy certain things, and the trustee then decides whether the requests meet the conditions of the trust and, thus, should be funded. While it's clear your child needs some spending money for groceries and such, the conditions of the trust dictate the acceptability of bigger-ticket items. By directly deciding on and buying those things for your child, rather than doling out a cash allowance, the trust ensures the beneficiary is well cared for without risking their cash assets rising above $2,000.

It's very typical for parents to serve as the trustees of the trust initially, as they want to steer the course of their child's financial plan while they're still alive. After they die, administration often falls to a healthy sibling or other trusted family member. Keep in mind, however, the administration of trusts can cause rifts within families. The mentally ill child can start to view the trustee sibling as the "bad guy" for turning down requests for money outside the bounds of the trust. As a result, I often recommend family members be cotrustees with a corporate entity. Under those circumstances, the third party can be the "bad guy" blamed for turning down requests, which avoids a great deal of conflict among family members. Hiring a corporate trustee costs money, though, and not all the fees are the same. Do your research before pursuing that route.

In reality, anyone can serve as a trustee, including a lawyer or a trusted family friend. There are corporate entities that specialize in administering trusts, and some of them are very good at what they do. The best choice depends on your specific goals and financial constraints.

## POOLED TRUSTS

The two types of trusts I described above, first-party and

third-party, are private trusts. Private trusts are known as (d)(4)(A) trusts because of the section of federal law spelling out their rules. An attorney sets up a private trust to benefit your child alone. Your child is the sole beneficiary—it doesn't benefit anyone else.

The other option is a pooled trust, known as (d)(4)(C); you pool your money for investment purposes with other people in your situation whom you don't know, through a nonprofit entity. The nonprofit writes and administers the trust and maintains separate accounts for each beneficiary's needs. By contributing funds, new beneficiaries add themselves to the pooled trust and essentially become subscribers. Because the trust document has already been written, there is less flexibility than if you'd structured your own trust, but the process is less expensive. The nonprofit generally charges an annual fee as a percentage of the assets you're contributing. This fee can vary, so it's important to do your research about the options available and their costs. As everywhere else, you want the lowest fee possible—in concert, here, with a trustee you believe will do a good job.

A pooled trust is a good option when you want the structure of a trust to protect your child but don't want to worry about creating the document and designating the trustee, or don't have a lot of assets to contribute. The nonprofit already has the structure in place, so you can simply join.

Again, you'll want to do your research. Find out who the cotrustees are and how many of them there are. You'll want to know why they're serving as trustees and what their areas of expertise are with regard to special needs, finance, government benefits eligibility, and so on. Different trustees specialize in different special needs, such as mental illness or autism. You'll want to pick a trust that's familiar with the unique considerations relevant to your child's condition.

A pooled trust can potentially give you access to more investment vehicles, but you're constrained by the trust's choice of those vehicles, the strategy, and the cost of the trust. You aren't going to be interacting with or steering the direction of the trust's financial manager, as you could with a private trust—you're just adding your child as a beneficiary. As with ABLE accounts, not all pooled trusts are created equal. Some are much better than others. In order to ensure you choose wisely, one good place to start your research is the website of the Academy of Special Needs Planners (ASNP), an organization made up almost entirely of lawyers. The site lists the options by state. You'll want to choose a pooled trust in your state because Medicaid rules are state-specific.

By putting your money in a pooled trust, you're at the mercy of its administration. Its strategy could change over time. So in addition to doing research online, if I were in the situation of choosing a pooled trust, I would also drive to the office and meet in person with the trustees. I would have lunch with them and ask them a lot of pointed questions. I'd be considering the granular details of their approach as well as doing a gut check regarding my overall impression of the operation. What safety valves are in place? What assurances and guarantees do you have that the trust will continue to operate in your child's best interests?

## CHOOSING BETWEEN PRIVATE AND POOLED TRUSTS

Pooled trusts are already established, which is great if you don't have a team of legal and financial experts in place and don't want to go through the process of assembling one. They're also more economical if you only have a relatively small amount of money to protect. Many investment advisors require a minimum amount of $500,000 or more, so a pooled trust would be a way to get big money management ability with a smaller amount.

Pooled trusts offer the convenience of having all the details taken care of for you, but the trade-off is that you're subject to whatever investment approach the managers decide to take. As a financial advisor, I would particularly scrutinize a pooled trust's investment strategy. To make the most of your money, it's important to invest efficiently and only expose yourself to risks that can be supported by academic evidence. Before choosing a pooled trust, it might be prudent to consult with a neutral financial professional who isn't associated with the trust. That person could dig into the financial specifics for you so that you can make an informed decision.

On the other hand, if you have a larger amount of money to put in a trust, the upfront cost of having a lawyer draw up a tailored, private agreement might not be significant compared to the value of your assets. The customization and power to set your own structure, trustees, investment strategy, and so on might be worth the initial effort and cost. You can also find a fiduciary financial advisor that you trust to administer the investments in the way you choose, an additional benefit.

If you've funded your child's ABLE account close to the $100,000 maximum and have only $30,000 or so left over, then a pooled trust makes a lot of sense. It's an efficient way to take advantage of economies of scale by splitting legal, administrative, and tax-preparation costs with other members of the pool. If you fund the ABLE account and still have, say, $500,000 to put away for your child, then having an attorney draw up appropriate private first- and third-party trusts could be worth the cost. I often recommend private trusts for large amounts of money, and pooled trusts (with research) for smaller amounts, but there is a gray in-between where parents should use discretion based on their goals. It's there that talking to a qualified fiduciary financial planner or lawyer with expertise in special needs trusts can be most helpful.

## TRUSTS PROTECT PEOPLE WITH SPECIAL NEEDS

People with mental illness can be targets for a predator looking to con them out of their money. A trustee provides a safeguard. A financial predator can't just sell a story to the beneficiary and walk away with the money—they'd have to persuade the trustee, too. Because a responsible sibling or fiduciary corporate entity wouldn't sign off on some harebrained scheme, the funds in the trust are protected.

Furthermore, trusts are creditor-proof. The funds in the trust fall outside the general estate, so if your child does something that gets them sued or results in a financial judgment against them, creditors cannot take the money in the trust. Again, this protects the beneficiary while giving you peace of mind about the security of the plan for your child's care. People with mental illness don't always make decisions in their own best interests, so having a trustee to manage their funds ensures someone else will look out for them.

## NOT OFFERING LEGAL ADVICE

I want to be clear that I'm not offering legal advice. I'm not an attorney. I can't possibly speak to the details of every reader's unique situation, and I'm not experienced with the laws of every state. For any legal questions, please seek the counsel of an attorney in your state who specializes in special needs trusts. The ASNP lists qualified lawyers by state as well. My purpose in this chapter is to explain why you might want to consider setting up special needs trusts, to outline some of the options, and to raise some of the questions you might want to answer with the help of a qualified lawyer.

## THE BANANA TRUST

To give you an idea of how trusts can work in practice, I'll tell you the story of a family I worked with. The clients had immigrated to the United States and had previously operated a banana plantation in their home country. They set up what they called The Banana Trust (the fruit name has been changed to protect confidentiality!). There were three kids, and the oldest daughter acted as cotrustee with a corporate trustee. The corporate trustee was there to be the enforcer, to ensure the trust's guidelines were followed and the trust's tax returns were filed on time, and so on. The daughter, in turn, benefitted from professional advice and signed off on decisions. She was also able to keep an eye on the corporate trustee in order to ensure he acted in the best interests of all the siblings. The arrangement required that two trustees had to be in agreement on decisions, so both could monitor the other.

The brother decided he had to have a Corvette. The older sister thought this was a complete waste of money, especially considering his driving habits. But she knew she couldn't just say no and keep a good relationship with him. Having the corporate trustee allowed her to commiserate with her brother and blame the denial on a neutral third party by saying, "I'm sorry, but the trustee doesn't agree that this is of benefit to you." The brother wasn't happy but had no choice but to accept the answer. Having two trustees kept the process running smoothly financially and emotionally within the family.

Later that year, the sister talked to a friend whose parents had left a trust to him alone. He was literally having trouble sleeping, up nights worrying about the tremendous weight of responsibility they'd left him. She didn't lose sleep at all, she realized. When she had a question or needed help, the corporate trustee was there. The sister was there to make sure her parent's wishes for their money were followed, but she could still get along with her siblings, and still have a life without all that extra weight. Her parents had been incredibly wise, and she realized more and more how grateful she was to them for that wisdom as time went on.

## TRUSTS AND ABLE ACCOUNTS COMPLEMENT EACH OTHER

The ABLE account is a great way to get started with financial planning for your child's future. It's an existing structure you can get started with right away, without having to invest a lot of money in document preparation or meetings with a lawyer. Since you are limited to funding the ABLE account with $15,000 per year, it'll take you some time until the account approaches the $100,000 limit. The ABLE plan is a convenient, flexible, trustee-free tool to benefit your child, and you can keep using it forever. Adding the trust, which has no practical limit to its possible assets, means you can continue the estate- and financial-planning process as far as you need to. Keep in mind the ABLE account belongs to your child—they have access to it without you or a trustee signing off on it. That in itself may be a reason you skip the ABLE account or keep the funding low and focus on building assets in either a first-party or third-party special needs trust. But if you're comfortable with your child having direct access to funds, an ABLE account is often the right first step.

## ANOTHER TOOL IN THE FINANCIAL TOOLBOX

Trusts offer a useful advanced-planning component of an affluent family's financial strategy, ensuring the appropriate disposition of the estate and funding the ongoing care of their children. Trusts prevent eligibility issues regarding government benefits. They provide a place for life insurance proceeds to go. You can put your house in a trust, ensuring your child has a stable roof over their head when you're gone. If the trust sells the house, the funds stay in the trust, so the assets continue to receive the oversight of a fiduciary trustee. Life insurance and real estate represent many people's largest assets, and a trust is a strategic way to protect their value and use it to maintain a good quality of life for a child with special needs.

## GUIDANCE FOR SETTING UP A SPECIAL NEEDS TRUST

Here's my main piece of advice regarding setting up a special needs trust: don't do it yourself. I know there are websites that talk about how to write a third-party trust yourself, but I don't think it's a good idea. Anything you get off the internet or out of a book will be boilerplate language that might not be a good fit for your situation, and you may not fully understand it.

If you try to create a trust on your own, you also won't have the benefit of experienced professionals digging deep into your situation and asking the right questions. You won't know what you don't know, and that can have negative consequences for your overarching goal: planning for the care of your child. I highly recommend a qualified lawyer experienced in special needs trusts, ideally in concert with your financial advisor's input. I've found the team approach works best, and that's why my firm emphasizes assembling relevant experts for our clients and helping coordinate those relationships.

## FUNDING THE TRUST

A third-party special needs trust can be funded by the parents' assets, either by titling assets to the trust now or by designating the trust to receive their assets upon their deaths. Life insurance or gifts from other family members can fund a trust. Assets in the child's name can also be used to fund a first-party special needs trust. Be careful not to commingle assets belonging to parents and children, because as I mentioned previously, all the money is then subject to Medicaid payback upon the child's death. It's better to set up a first-party trust for the child's assets and a third-party trust for everything else to allow for excess money to be passed down to additional members of the family when no longer needed. Consult with an experienced lawyer in your state to determine how this would work in your particular case.

## HOW MUCH LIFE INSURANCE IS ENOUGH?

If you don't have sufficient assets from other sources, life insurance can be a great way to fund a trust. The exact amount you need will depend entirely on the specifics of your situation. You need to ask yourself what realistic standard of living you want to ensure for your child. What will their needs be beyond their government benefits? Then, you need to calculate how much money it would take to achieve that standard of living. What is the monthly price tag for what you want your child to have? Given a conservative estimate of investment returns, how much money would have to be in the trust in order to cover that monthly price tag? Once you have that information, you can evaluate how much money you have already and then use life insurance to cover the shortfall.

For instance, you might want your child to have access to $5,000 a month for the rest of their life. Given their age and health as well as estimates of returns on investment, you might determine you need $1.5 million. If you only have $850,000 with which to fund the trust, you could make up the shortfall by buying $650,000 of life insurance payable to the trust when the first parent dies. That way, the trust will be fully funded to meet your goal. I can't prescribe a number to you, because I don't know your situation, what other funds you have, what your goals are, or what your child's needs are. But I can recommend you take all the issues I've listed into consideration in order to determine an appropriate policy amount.

Life insurance is a way of buying a big chunk of future money for less than the value of that money at the time of purchase. You should be following a sound strategy to calculate the size of your purchase. Some people simply buy the biggest, roundest number they can afford at the time, or they buy far too little for their goals. When someone tells me they only have $250,000 in life insurance, I often dig deeper and find they don't have a systematic plan for covering all the costs that led them to buy the policy in the first place. On the other hand, someone might tell me they have $1 million in life insurance, but they're not able to explain why. They just bought a big policy because they thought they were supposed to. Once I have a complete picture of a client's current policies and assets as well as their goals, I can help adjust the policy amounts so they serve a concrete purpose.

It's important to be realistic about the standard of living you want for your child and how much it will cost. A big trust account will not be enough if costs outstrip the funds available. Conversely, when used wisely, a smaller amount of money can go a long way toward a modest standard of living.

Spending less than you bring in leaves a cushion that can compound through investing. That's also true after your death as your child spends what you have left to him or her; controlled spending lets the money last so much longer. The same, however, goes for saving while your child is still alive. If you make $10,000 a month and only spend

$6,500 on a great, intentional lifestyle, there's money left over to save and invest to fund the trust. If you make $15,000 a month but spend like you've made $30,000, you're going to go broke, and there won't be anything left for your child. No two clients are the same in their values, in what they can save, and in their personal definition of what is "enough" for both themselves and their child. I recommend finding a professional advisor with a depth and breadth of experience working with many different kinds of clients. That advisor can help you identify your core goals and the strategy best needed to accumulate the money you'll need to meet those goals.

## MY "RULE," AKA "THE COCKTAIL NAPKIN RESPONSE"

I can't give you a definitive rule for approaching your finances, because I don't know the details of your situation. However, if I were at a cocktail party and someone pressed me to give a general place to start, I would give the 4 percent rule: your child's budget for the year should be 4 percent of their total available assets. For example, if you want them to have access to $10,000 per year, there should be $250,000 in the account, because $10,000 is 4 percent of $250,000. If you want them to have $50,000 per year, then there should be $1.25 million in the account.

My "rule" assumes you have a low-cost, diversified portfolio invested in global capital markets, for the reasons outlined in the chapter on investing. If your portfolio is not well diversified across global capital markets, then you may want to limit the annual distribution to something less than 4 percent of the total portfolio value. I'm also assuming you want the portfolio to last indefinitely.

If your desired annual distribution requires more money than you have in assets, then you need to determine the best way to address the shortfall in your particular situation. As we've talked about, life insurance can be a good way to make up the difference because it costs pennies on the dollar.

## AVOID THE COMMON MISTAKE OF UNDERFUNDING

People often underfund their trusts because they don't do the math correctly. When determining the projected annual distribution for your child, keep in mind inflation continues to increase the cost of living. The long-term average my firm currently uses to estimate inflation is 3.76 percent annually. I've seen models that use numbers as high as 4.12 percent. It's better to overestimate inflation than underestimate it if you want to ensure your child has enough assets to maintain an adequate level of purchasing power over time. Medical costs also continue to increase on the order of 5 percent annually (more than inflation). You'll want to research and factor in the long-term average increase in this sector, as your child with special needs will likely need access to comprehensive medical care for many years and will need to be able to afford it.

With all the projections I'm covering here, it's important to calculate based on historical trends. Don't make the mistake of underfunding because you're taking a leap of faith that medical increases will drop to 3 percent annually when they've always been closer to 5 percent.

As you're estimating your money's growth through investments over time, you should also use relatively conservative projections of returns. Some people are unrealistic when estimating how much their assets will grow. You might research ten-year stock market average returns and see numbers like 9.5 or 10 percent, but my firm does not expose our clients' portfolios to that level of risk. A more realistic estimate would be 6 percent, and a conservative number might be closer to 4 or 5 percent.

It's also common for people to fail to fund their trust at all. They have a lawyer draw up a sound legal document, but then they don't transfer any assets into it. They might feel good about the balance in their investment account but not realize they've failed to title the account to the trust or to name the trust as the beneficiary. There's no benefit to setting up a trust if you don't fund it!

A good financial advisor can help you navigate all the potential pitfalls I've listed here and more. They can also show you how different variables affect your bottom line, such as 3 percent inflation versus 5 percent inflation. Taking into account the different possible outcomes based on these variables, you can work together to chart a path that maximizes your chances of success in meeting your goals.

## FAMILY GIFTS

Once you've established a third-party special needs trust, let family members know that this is where they should send gifts. It's common to lose eligibility for government benefits because of mishandling big gifts, and you don't want that to happen to you. The trust is there to ensure the child's assets don't exceed the legal maximums—use it!

Once again, you're giving your child an amazing gift of both money and love by funding a trust for their future needs. By doing so in a way that keeps them eligible for government benefits, you maximize their future financial security. Good planning now gives your child the best possible future, and you should be proud of the work you're doing to ensure it.

# CHAPTER EIGHT

---

# Taking Care of the Parent

I have a client who was so focused on saving and living frugally that I finally had to tell her to start spending her money. She had more than enough to do anything she wanted, but she needed a nudge to start taking care of herself. Instead of focusing on the investment strategy, I asked her an essential question from back in the discovery process, "What's on your bucket list?"

The issue of self-care is particularly important for parents of children with mental illness. If you focus only on saving money and caring for your child, you will burn out. I can see it in my wife's face when she's exhausted and needs a break. We've cultivated a support system so a family friend can drop by in the evening and ensure my son takes his medication if we're away. We'll also use a professional respite care worker on occasion if we're going to be gone for a few days. Recharging helps us and our son.

Sometimes, clients seem to need my blessing in order to spend on themselves, whether it's to take a vacation or to take care of themselves in another way. This chapter is my official blessing to do what you need to do, not only to take care of your child, but to take care of yourself. Everyone will do better when you take care of yourself.

## A TOLL ON THE BODY, MIND, AND HEART

It's important to keep tabs on your energy levels because mental and physical exhaustion get in the way of making even small decisions. During the discovery process with a new client who has a child with mental illness, often the client's stress and fatigue become obvious. They don't directly tell me they need time to recover and recharge or that they need time alone and away from their child with mental illness. I can see from their eyes and their demeanor they're burning out.

In the beginning, when your child is first diagnosed and in crisis, there isn't much opportunity for a break. Sometimes, the only chance to catch your breath is when they're hospitalized. Even though you don't want them to get to that point, it's normal to feel a sense of relief when they're away and you have a pause in the intense demands. When my son has been away, we've noticed how quiet the house is. It gives us a chance to get his room clean and livable again. We can take a moment for ourselves.

In working with my clients, part of our path together is to figure out how to build in breaks and self-care. Yes, it's important to set clear financial goals and follow a systematic plan to save for them. One of the goals we have to build in, though, is caring for the parents. If we're not careful, the child can become the focus to the exclusion of everything and everyone else.

People with mental illness are hospitalized because they reach a crisis point and are in a psychotic state. Making the choice as a parent to call the police and hospitalize your child against their will is extremely taxing. When the police come, your child is likely to yell and curse at you as if you're the worst person in the world. Most patients who reach the point of needing hospitalization present a danger to themselves, not other people. You're committing them for their own safety. Even though it's the right thing to do, it's a gut-wrenching situation. It's normal to know the decision is the right one, and yet to struggle with it emotionally. At those times, more than any others, it's important to take time for self-care.

## CARING FOR YOURSELF

There are huge long-term negative impacts for stress and sleep deprivation. Many of my clients are firefighters. They spend twenty-five years or more sleep-deprived, because that's just part of the job. They exist in a state of extreme mental and physical stress that starts to seem normal. There are consequences, though. According to a 2015 article published in the *Journal of Emergency Medical Services*, and a survey of more than four thousand first responders, the rate of attempted suicide among first responders is more than ten times higher than the general population. All too often they take their own lives after they've retired.

Parents of adult children with mental illness also live in a state of stress and sleep deprivation for years, and we should take that seriously. While it may feel selfish to take time for yourself to destress, or especially to sleep, if you have a heart attack, become obese, get diabetes, develop early onset dementia, or become compromised by some other stress-related condition, you will not be as able to care for your child. Self-preservation isn't selfish—it's about being around for the long haul.

Your child's diagnosis doesn't make your other responsibilities go away. If they're up all night, you're likely up as well—but you still have to go to work. I've spent many sleepless nights attending to my son's needs or hearing him bang around the house. It's hard to sleep through. Still, I need to find ways to take care of myself so that I can continue doing my job, supporting him, and supporting myself and the rest of my family. Sleep isn't optional, and neither is self-care.

## CARING FOR YOUR RELATIONSHIP

In addition to taking care of yourself, if you're married or in a long-term relationship, it's important to take care of that relationship, too. After my son had been diagnosed, my wife and I started drifting apart. We were so preoccupied with him, we weren't investing in our relationship. She was the one to tell me we needed to go to a therapist, and I'm very glad she did. We were able to reconnect with each other and what we needed as a couple, which, in turn, made us an unstoppable, healthy team to care for our son.

By contrast, we're friends with a couple whose child has the same diagnosis as ours, and they have not invested in their marriage. The wife has confided in me that she feels she doesn't exist in the relationship anymore because her husband is so focused on their son. She'd like to go on a vacation, just the two of them, to recharge and have a change of scenery. Even when their son was hospitalized for six months, he insisted on visiting every day. It's great that he cares about their son so much, but the intense focus on only him is breeding dependence in the child and estrangement in the marriage.

You do not want to add divorce to all the other chaos going on in your life if you can help it. Taking care of yourself and your romantic relationship creates a firm foundation from which to care for your child. If you aren't healthy, grounded, and functioning as well as you can, then you're not going to have the emotional and psychological resources to advocate and plan for your child's future.

## BE PROACTIVE AND BUILD COMMUNITY

It's unlikely anyone will step in and say to you, "You look stressed. Why don't you go take a two-week vacation while I look after your kid?" To get that kind of help, you'll need a strong community, and you'll have to ask. For some people, including my wife and me, faith communities offer a strong support system. We're Unitarian Universalists, so the members of our church run the gamut from atheists to strong believers in God. The thing we all have in common is wanting a spiritual connection and a strong network of caring people. Whatever your background, I'd recommend you take the time to establish a strong, caring community of support—it's absolutely essential for your own health.

I love sailing more than almost any other activity. My son

hasn't been able to join us on sailing trips because it feels too confining to him, and there's no way to return home quickly if he gets into a crisis state. Even so, my wife and I were able to take a two-week sailing trip while ensuring his care. We reached out to our support network and asked for help. Different people were able to come by in the morning and evening to ensure he took his medication. Other people could come spend some time with him in the afternoon. He received so much attention that he actually told some people he appreciated what they were doing, but he was wondering if they could leave! In other words, he was not in any way neglected—and we were able to recharge.

Building deep, strong friendships takes time. You need to know people well enough to trust them with your child's care, and they need to know you well enough to be willing to do you some huge favors. In our case, it took many years of knowing people through our church before we got to that point. You don't have to be part of a faith community to have a support system—I just know that faith communities tend to emphasize mutual assistance and service. If you're looking for secular resources, NAMI and other support groups can be good places to start meeting people and building relationships. The important thing to keep in mind is you cannot care for your child entirely alone without burning out.

I'll close with this thought: a good financial advisor can

also play an important role in helping you take care of yourself. He or she will go beyond crunching numbers and understand that your money needs to serve you and your goals, including ensuring your health and well-being. He or she can become almost like a trusted friend who can see how you're doing and nudge you to take some time and resources to recharge when you need it.

## FINANCIAL CONSIDERATIONS RELATED TO CARING FOR YOURSELF AS A PARENT

Caring for your child and yourself can be expensive. If you need a break and don't have favors you can call in with your community, you may need to pay for respite care or hire an ongoing helper to assist your child in your home. Regardless of your situation, I would encourage you to keep an eye out for opportunities to recharge and seize them.

For example, when your child is hospitalized, that can be a good opportunity to catch up on your own needs. In Florida, people with mental illness can be involuntarily committed for seventy-two hours under the Baker Act when they pose a danger to themselves or others. Once, when our son was going through a particularly difficult period, he was taken to the hospital under the Baker Act. Gayle and I had had many sleepless nights and incredible worry about our son in the weeks leading up to his committal. We were exhausted. So we told the staff at the hospital we were going away for some much-needed rest, and we made sure they had our contact information. They understood we'd come back at a moment's notice if they had any concern. We then spent the next few days at the beach and got a much-needed recharge time that helped us come back ready to support our son as he transitioned back into normal life. The takeaway lesson is to use the opportunities and resources at your disposal. Take advantage of the time you have, even if it's unexpected.

## LONG-TERM CARE INSURANCE

I also encourage caregivers to consider long-term care insurance for themselves. This insurance is especially important for those with moderate to lower levels of assets and investments compared to their spending needs. As I've discussed, caregiving takes a physical, mental, and emotional toll on the caregiver. If you end up with a health problem, who will take care of you? Long-term care policies provide an income stream so that someone can take care of you if you need it. Such insurance tends to define a qualifying "long-term care event" by looking at six activities of daily living. The policy pays out when you can't do at least two of them on your own: eating, bathing, dressing, toileting, transferring, and continence.

Long-term care insurance can be quite expensive as the

incidence of claims is quite high and the cost of each claim could potentially be in the hundreds of thousands of dollars. However, ensuring your own care is covered, if needed, it protects you and your assets long-term. If you can no longer work or take care of yourself, you don't want to end up in a position where you can't pay your mortgage or afford the in-home assistance you need. The cost of care can vary widely by region. In our area of South Florida, on the low end, around-the-clock care could cost $5,000 to $6,000 a month—that's up to $72,000 a year in expenses on top of all the bills you already had to pay. Having a financial plan to pay for your needs in the event of a major health event, which is more likely given the stress you're under, helps protect your child financially, too.

If your portfolio is large enough to cover in-home care in addition to all your other expenses and those of your child (this varies depending on your needs, but starts at about $2.5 to $3 million in assets), then you can "self-insure" and you don't need to buy the insurance. Many people don't have that much of a cushion in their investment assets, though. In that case, long-term care insurance can prevent a budget shortfall. In purchasing this kind of insurance, you have a couple of options.

One, you can buy a stand-alone policy. In that scenario, you pay a monthly premium to keep the policy in effect until there's a qualifying event. A policy that covers *all* the costs associated with a long-term care event for an extended period of time could be quite pricey and might not work with your budget. In that case, you can still get coverage that would provide a supplement to your income, even if it wouldn't cover all your costs. Just as in the case of special needs trusts, it's better to have some additional money available if needed than to have none at all. If you can't afford a policy that would pay $250 a day for the rest of your life, maybe you could afford coverage that would pay out $100 a day for three years in the event you need it. Something is better than nothing.

Another option is to purchase life insurance with a long-term care benefit rider. These types of life insurance policies are becoming more common as insurers are seeking alternative ways to provide this important benefit. With this type of product, you transfer a significant amount of cash—perhaps $25,000 to $100,000—to the policy. Sometimes, you also pay a monthly amount to get to the benefit level you're seeking. The policy carries a death benefit, a long-term care benefit, and a cash value. We've found clients like these types of policies because they feel as if, one way or another, they or their family is going to benefit from them. If they decide to discontinue coverage, they can usually get most if not all their money back out of the policy. If they have a qualifying long-term care event, the policy pays for their care. If they die, the policy pays their beneficiary. My clients have been increasingly interested in long-term care riders for this reason. They don't want to waste their money buying an expensive policy they might never use. But, they like the idea that if they don't use it, it will pay money out to their family or their trust when they die. With a rider, your family benefits whether you need the long-term care or not.

## MY SELF-CARE RECOMMENDATIONS

Caring for a child with mental illness carries with it a huge number of regular stressors, and as such, I can't emphasize enough how important it is to take care of yourself along the way. Part of your responsibility as a parent is to plan ahead and take care of yourself so you can be there for your child over the long haul. Catch up on sleep as much as you can whenever you can. Eat a healthy diet. Socialize with friends, and build a support network through a caring community. Attend support-group meetings through NAMI, MHA, or another organization of people who truly understand. Support groups help you see you're not alone—other parents of kids with special needs are going through very similar experiences. You can help one another.

Mental illness carries an undeniable stigma, so it's often tempting to keep to yourself. Don't. Shame isolates us from each other, keeps parents from getting the support they need, and even prevents people with mental illness from seeking essential treatment. You cannot take care of yourself by yourself, and isolation will only make your struggles worse. There are people out there whose energy, experiences, and ideas can benefit you. By talking about what you're going through, with people who understand and with a loving community, you're able to receive the support you'll need to make it over the long term.

My wife recommends building creativity and meaning into your life. For her, that means advocacy. She doesn't just take care of the day-to-day needs of our son—she also devotes energy to making the world a better place for so many people like him. She's able to channel her talent and quest for meaning into advocating at the state level, which keeps her engaged with and involved in a sphere bigger than just our family.

My wife's work has connected her with people we can help and people who can help us. As of this writing, she's recently been interviewed by ABC News. ABC's piece focused on the discussion around mental illness with regard to mass shootings—and the fact that most people with a mental illness are actually in danger of harming themselves, not being violent toward others. People in the mental health community know the political emphasis on linking mental illness to violence is largely inaccurate and misleading. We know my son is a sensitive, intelligent individual who cannot be summed up by the popular stereotypes of schizophrenia. Speaking publicly allows us to help correct the misconceptions.

The interview was a kind of coming out. Instead of hiding, my wife and I are raising our voices in ways that work for us, and we have included our son in the process. Going public on our own terms is an antidote to stigma. There will always be insensitive people in the world, and we have to be strong enough not to get derailed by their insensitivity. As it turns out, the response to our sharing has been overwhelmingly positive.

Don't be afraid to spend time on yourself. In fact, I think it's critical to both your mental health and to your child's. Get some exercise as regularly as you can, something you enjoy and that you can make part of your regular routine. Spend whatever time you can on a hobby. Make sure it's something you have passion for and find joy in doing. Having these moments of joy in your life keeps you strong when things get rough. They give you something to look forward to when you need it the most. And that's not just good for you—it's good for your child.

CHAPTER NINE

---

# The Financial Advisor at Thirty Thousand Feet

A client I'll call Harold came to me after working with a different financial advisor. After we looked at his portfolio, I could see all kinds of conflicts and mistakes in the investment strategy. His costs were much higher than they should be, and his allocation suggested his advisor had a poor academic understanding of how asset classes work together. I believe he could have been taking less risk in order to get the same return, and he could have been netting more of that return after expenses. To me, the portfolio looked like a typical one sold on the commission-incentivized "dark side," and ultimately it was not serving his needs the way it should have been.

I've found there's nothing to gain by criticizing someone's

previous advisor. Instead, I took Harold through the deep-dive discovery process that we do with all our clients. I outlined my firm's global, diversified asset-allocation strategy and provided him with the academic research backing up our approach. As a result, he came to the realization on his own that I knew what I was talking about, and that what he'd been doing wasn't the best way to achieve his goals. His advisor had been a nice person but hadn't had an effective, comprehensive strategy to managing his portfolio.

When we got to the end of the discovery meeting, he told me I now probably knew him better than anyone on the planet. He'd never told all of this detailed personal information to the same person before, and he was impressed I'd been able to get him to speak so freely. He was also putting me on notice: he recognized how much information he had given and was trusting me now to act in his best interest.

## IS A FINANCIAL ADVISOR NECESSARY?

I'm obviously biased as to the benefits of financial advisors, because I've devoted my professional life to serving clients. To try to determine whether a financial advisor is appropriate for your particular situation and goals, I would encourage you to ask yourself where your energy is best spent. We all have a finite amount of energy, and we all have to prioritize. If you are caring for a child with mental illness, you're already wrapped up in the day-to-day demands of that responsibility. You likely do not have energy to spare, not if you're also making the essential time to care for yourself. Is doing your financial planning and keeping up with investment theory yourself really the best use of your time and energy?

From my perspective, delegating financial management to a professional advisor is a sound decision that can pay for itself many times over. A good advisor will prevent common mistakes of do-it-yourself portfolio management, such as ineffective diversification or getting jittery about a down market and pulling your money out at the wrong time. If you sell at the wrong time, the money is gone. You no longer have the shares to benefit from a market rebound. Avoiding such a loss even once can save enough money to pay for many, many years of professional advice. Regardless of your specific financial situation, a knowledgeable advisor can save you valuable time and give you peace of mind.

Advisors can also provide a great antidote to financial procrastination. They know how to create appropriate, actionable plans, and they manage the schedule necessary to implement those plans. At the end of your discovery meeting, your advisor will schedule a follow-up. It's kind of like going to the dentist. How many of us would get our teeth cleaned as often as we need to if the office didn't make our next appointment before we left the last one? I know I wouldn't—I hate going to the dentist.

For some people, dealing with financial issues is about as fun as dealing with tooth decay. An experienced professional can help coach you through the initial discomfort so that you can start building and managing the financial resources you need to achieve your big goals. The gains you make over time more than justify that discomfort at the beginning.

Furthermore, you're understandably emotionally invested in your money and situation. Because of this, it can be helpful to work with someone who has a level of professional detachment. Good advisors don't let emotions pull them away from what research and evidence indicate is the best course. We focus on giving solid advice and helping our clients make steady progress.

In addition, a good financial advisor helps find and manage a team of relevant professionals so you don't have to. No one can be an expert in every subject area. Building a successful financial plan is like building a house. A single contractor doesn't do everything, but rather works with a plumber, an electrician, a drywaller, a painter, a roofer, and so on. A good financial advisor is like the general contractor who finds the best subcontractors. In the case of your plan, those subcontractors are likely a lawyer, an accountant, a life insurance representative, a long-term care insurance representative, and so on.

Delegating to experts allows for better efficacy and efficiency. Instead of learning everything yourself and risking managing at least part of your plan poorly, you can be confident someone with the right specialty is overseeing each angle. It's theoretically possible to manage everything on your own, but it's more effective to have help. A financial advisor can assemble a team of the right professionals, ones who have a proven track record and will work together toward your common goals efficiently.

## THE ROLE OF A FINANCIAL ADVISOR

Like a good CFO, the financial advisor's job is not to make all the decisions but rather to ensure that you, as CEO, have accurate data and guidance so that the appropriate decision becomes clear. The process is collaborative. Your advisor might bring up a decision you need to make, and you might not even have realized until then that you needed to make it. Your advisor can also inform you of possible consequences of different decisions and suggest solutions based on solid research. That's the benefit of professionals; they can help you uncover what you don't know. Ultimately, however, your portfolio is your money, so you call the shots.

As a financial advisor, I observe each client's process from thirty thousand feet. We might think of it like this: my client is down on the ground in the midst of their own life, while I'm above with a bird's-eye view. I can see all the elements of their financial landscape to figure out what's happening and what needs to be done. I can see that the client needs to write a trust, do their taxes, and get a certain kind of life insurance. I don't get down on the ground and handle all those things myself, but my perspective allows me to see who is doing what and where the plan is headed. From the ground, the client can't crane their neck to keep track of the lawyer and the accountant at the same time, but from up above, I can.

Having a financial advisor's high-level perspective is like being in the club seats at a hockey game. My wife never enjoyed hockey, because she couldn't keep track of where the puck was. She saw people skating one place or another and didn't really understand why. When we sat in the club seats, though, we were up high. From there, she could see what was happening with the puck, why people were doing what they were doing, and how the pieces all fit together. The perspective let her understand what was going on and enjoy the game.

From thirty thousand feet, I can see what's coming on the horizon and help plan for it. I can't predict exactly what will happen with a given market at a certain time, but I can see when someone's investment strategy exposes them to risks that can be eliminated or mitigated. I can see when they have a lot of assets but no trust to transfer them in a strategic way. I can see when they don't have sufficient protection to prevent heavy losses in the case of a lawsuit. I can help my clients plan for the future and adapt their approach as their lives and the lives of their children change.

My strategy is proactive rather than reactive. While sometimes we have to react to unanticipated events, in most cases, we can plan ahead. We know retirement is coming, and we know there will be a market correction at some point. We can diversify and balance the portfolio so that the client is prepared.

I surround each client, depending on their goals and needs, with a team of competent professionals on the ground—a lawyer, an accountant, and so on. I have a dual role: I spend some time on the ground as the investment consultant, with my own specialized up-close view, and then I go back to the air to regularly check on the advancement of the entire plan.

I've seen some groups of professionals who should be working as a team but actually have a very adversarial relationship, because no one is up in the air serving as the lead advisor. If everyone is trying to be the quarterback or striking out on their own without adhering to a cohesive strategy, the client is the one who loses out. For example, some CPAs also sell financial products, which I see as a conflict of interest and something that would easily lead to conflicts with the investment manager. Or, a lawyer might want to set up a trust while the accountant pushes for a more complex retirement plan using the same resources. Understandably, clients working with a fractured team start to distrust the process and the individual experts, because they're contradicting each other and failing to get the job done.

To encourage collaboration and avoid internal conflicts, a good financial advisor will get input from the various team members and then present it to the client in an organized and prioritized fashion. Once the client agrees to a direction, the advisor will follow up and ensure everyone is moving in that direction. Cohesion both fosters the client's trust and ensures the client's true financial needs are met consistently.

Unfortunately, financial advisors with the experience and ability to take on such a leadership role are relatively rare. When I first founded my firm, we followed a more traditional model—we helped with investments and then referred to lawyers and other professionals as needed. The problem was that the process was inefficient and unpredictable for the clients. I wasn't collaborating directly with the other professionals, so sometimes our advice conflicted—and I didn't know this, because we weren't working together. I realized, instead, we needed to have a standard process with clear steps, meeting with the professional team in advance and then walking the client through the plan in stages. We moved to the process I outlined in a previous chapter, starting with investment consulting and then moving on to the advanced-planning elements. We tell clients from the beginning what our steps will be so they know what will happen next and can feel confident in our direction. Working directly with a team of professionals to ensure the client's plan is solid and coherent has led to dramatically better results, and we're very happy with this process.

Ideally, you can find yourself an empathetic, experienced advisor who is local to your area. It's hugely beneficial to meet with someone face-to-face. If that's not possible, my firm—Northstar Financial Planners in Fort Lauderdale—does meet with clients in other states. We go through the same discovery and advising process as we do in person, just using video conferencing and screen sharing.

## FINDING A FINANCIAL ADVISOR WHO MEETS YOUR UNIQUE NEEDS

Above all else, any financial advisor you choose must be a fiduciary. Very few advisors truly are, so you will need to weed out a lot of candidates based on that criterion alone. To be truly fiduciary, an advisor must eliminate sales incentives and conflicts of interest so that they can give you a wholly unbiased opinion that's in your best financial interest. Ask potential advisors directly if they are solely fiduciary advisors—and listen carefully to the responses. Advisors who try to play both sides of the fence with some fiduciary services and some sales-based services still have a bias. That disqualifies them immediately from serving your best interest. "Fee-based" is not the same as "fee-only." Ask the question, "Is 100 percent of your revenue from fees billed directly to clients?" If they can't answer yes, then move on.

For the purposes of our discussion, "fiduciary" and "fee-only" are essentially interchangeable. By charging a flat fee instead of getting a commission for selling certain products, an advisor can give you an honest opinion. It's like hiring a broker who has access to all the car makes available instead of someone who only works for Chevrolet or Toyota. The Chevy salesperson is going to try to sell you a Chevy no matter what, even if the Toyota would actually meet your specific needs better. In terms of financial advice, you want someone who can match you with the financial instruments that make the most sense for you specifically. You can do research on fee-only advisors in your area by going to NAPFA.org.

To return to the example of my client with the high-cost annuities, a fiduciary advisor would not have allowed her to get into that situation. She had purchased them while working with a commission-based advisor who had steered her toward products that would give him commissions. She could have had a portfolio with the same level of risk, potentially higher returns, and lower costs or, at the least, annuities without such high costs and exorbitant surrender fees. If she'd worked with a fee-only advisor from the beginning, her portfolio wouldn't have needed so much fixing.

## EXPERIENCE WITH MENTAL ILLNESS

In this book, I focus on parents or guardians of children who have mental illness. If that's your situation, it's critical to find an advisor who has experience with special needs and, if possible, with mental illness in particular. Someone who deeply understands your particular situation is going to give better advice. They'll be able to tailor their financial advice to you while also making appropriate recommendations for your larger situation, such as how to navigate government benefits and which other professionals would be of benefit to you. An advisor who has been personally impacted by family mental illness should have genuine empathy and a better understanding of how to deliver advice to you, too.

If you've been dealing with a child's mental illness, then

you've been through the wringer. You're likely stressed out, tired, and feeling beaten down. You may already have a sense you've made some financial mistakes or know you need help managing your finances better. When you're already feeling vulnerable, you don't want an uncaring advisor to start critiquing everything you've done wrong. An advisor who understands how draining it can be to manage special needs should frame his or her advice accordingly, focusing on supportive and constructive guidance. It's valuable to work with someone who can offer you kindness and understanding, and I'd suggest looking for those qualities in potential advisors.

At the same time, you want an advisor who will exhibit leadership and clarity. Kindness doesn't mean being wishy-washy. As I mentioned previously, many clients caring for children with mental illness need a financial advisor who can approach them in an almost paternal way—gentle but firm, keeping their best interests at the forefront. Many people are in their seventies by the time they start tackling their estates and their adult children's needs. They've needed help for a long time. Yes, they need an advisor who is nice, but that advisor also needs a rock-solid understanding of financial principles and must be able to communicate them in a direct and actionable way. Valuable advisors have a depth and breadth of experience with people in your situation. They can point out common pitfalls. They can tell if you're on a road that's headed off a cliff. On the ground, you likely can't see the cliff yet, but at thirty thousand feet, they can.

In this book, I've drawn from examples primarily with affluent families. If you have more limited means, though, you may still be able to benefit from consulting with an advisor. Depending on where you live and whom you talk to, you may experience some sticker shock when you hear the fees involved. If you're not used to hiring lawyers to draw up trusts, for example, it can sound like a lot of money. I would encourage you to consider the specifics of your situation and what the costs might be if you *don't* hire a professional. You may be able to meet with someone on an hourly basis to get some fundamental advice and then implement it yourself to save money. Also, I would encourage you not to be afraid to ask for an initial one-hour consultation. Many advisors on the fee-only side are fully aware they could make more money on commission, but instead, they've chosen to be in the business to help people. There are people out there who will meet with prospective clients and may be willing to give away some advice for free if the situation warrants it.

## KEY QUESTIONS TO ASK A POTENTIAL ADVISOR

When interviewing potential advisors, I would recommend asking a few key questions.

## HOW DO YOU WORK WITH YOUR CLIENTS?

An advisor worth working with will be able to explain a clear process to you. They should have a series of steps to uncover your goals, develop a plan, and implement that plan. They should have a team approach that enlists qualified professionals and manages those relationships for you. Most advisors want to give you a questionnaire, sell you some products, and manage your trusts. They tend to stop there, because they don't make commissions beyond that point, and that's not going to help you at all. A fiduciary advisor worth hiring will have a comprehensive, ongoing process to offer you. Keep looking until you find the right person.

## DO YOU HELP CLIENTS ADDRESS FINANCIAL GOALS BEYOND INVESTMENT?

I've never heard of a financial advisor who didn't do investment consulting. As the parent or guardian of a child with special needs, you need an advisor who offers advanced planning services as well (and I know of many advisors who don't do that). Will they help you enhance, manage, and protect your wealth? Do they have a go-to team of competent professionals who have experience with planning for mental health issues?

## DO YOU UNDERSTAND MY WORLD AND HAVE EXPERIENCE IN IT?

Your advisor doesn't necessarily have to be the parent of a child with the exact same diagnosis as yours. They should, however, have a thorough knowledge of planning for special needs and a familiarity with mental illness issues in particular. They should be able to give you sound financial advice and to incorporate empathy for your overall situation. Someone who understands your world and has relevant experience working with clients in your situation will be able to help you achieve your goals without you feeling constrained by stereotypes or stigma.

## DO YOU WORK WITH OUTSIDE SPECIALISTS?

Your advisor's firm does not need to focus entirely on mental health issues or even special needs more broadly. I certainly have clients who don't have children with special needs. The firm should, however, have a team of specialists experienced in this area to give you the best possible guidance for your situation. That team might be in-house or work in collaboration with other organizations and businesses.

## WHY DID YOU BECOME A FINANCIAL ADVISOR?

You'll need to do a gut check as you listen to an advisor's answer to the question. You want someone for whom advising is more than just a job and who will put your best interests first. Are they genuinely passionate about helping people, or did it just seem like the best way for them to make a lot of money? Do they just say the right words, or do you hear the passion in their voice? Normally a fiduciary advisor is there to help people, but you'll want to find one who you believe cares.

## ASK YOURSELF: IS WORKING WITH THIS PERSON A GOOD FINANCIAL DECISION?

Finally, in choosing an advisor, ask yourself whether you think you will look back in five to ten years and consider working with this particular person to be a good financial decision. At my firm, we go through a rediscovery process after working with a client for several years. We ask them the same questions from our initial meeting, including what their best and worst financial decisions have been. We frequently hear that working with our firm has been among our clients' best decisions. Of course, it makes me happy and proud to receive such positive feedback, but it also fills me with a sense of conviction that we offer a valuable, well-designed service. You'll want to work with someone who provokes just as much satisfaction in his or her clients as well.

I hope you'll use the questions above and the guidance in this book to make a similarly good choice for your own financial needs.

## THE BOTTOM LINE

When I think about the benefits of working with a financial advisor, the analogy comes to mind of doing your own dental work. Maybe you could find a way to do it, but it would be unpleasant and not very successful. There are tremendous benefits to *not* doing it yourself; a lot of very knowledgeable people still delegate their financial management. I know a Nobel laureate who uses a fee-only financial advisor, for example. I also know the CEO of what I consider to be one of the most reputable investment companies around, with Nobel Prize winners on its board. He taught me a tremendous amount about modern portfolio theory, and if anyone could manage their own portfolio, he could. However, he also uses a financial advisor. He understands the value of objective, third-party advice—the cost of paying a professional is worth it to him to get an outside perspective from someone who isn't so emotionally invested in his portfolio's performance.

Essentially the question becomes, Can you truly do it yourself? And even if you can, is this really what you want to spend your precious time on?

# Conclusion

## THERE IS GOOD NEWS HERE

Working with a competent professional financial advisor can be one of the best financial decisions you'll ever make. I've spoken to many people who say working with a financial advisor helped relieve them of worry, tension, and anxiety about their money and their future. Fear about the future comes from lacking a solid plan—a good financial advisor develops and helps to implement such a plan.

Worry about money often goes hand in hand with lack of planning and lack of knowledge; if you don't know where you are and where you're going, it's easy to have anxiety. My experience is that the worry of running out of money is not exclusive to people who don't have a lot of it. I've met people who have $5 million or more but are still worried about running out of money. By showing them how their assets compare to their lifestyle and goals, I can give them the reassurance they need to stop worrying. Even in the case of people with a little less built-in security, with a good plan and the reassurance of making steady progress toward that plan, most people are able to relax and enjoy life.

Once we've developed a plan, it's common for a client to go on autopilot for a while. What we came up with works well for them, and they don't have any major financial issues to worry about. Still, we like to rejuvenate the relationship and reevaluate the plan regularly. For some clients that may mean every year or two, while for others perhaps every five years. We'll have a rediscovery meeting during which we go back over their answers from our initial meeting. We ask them if anything has changed, particularly in the area of relationships. Even very important relationships may shift over time. A sister who was an integral part of their life might have become estranged during a dispute over their parents' estate, for example—such estrangements are common, unfortunately. If they previously set up a trust to benefit their sister but don't talk to her anymore, they might want to rethink that trust. On the happier side, the client may have a new child or grandchild who'll change the estate plan, or the client may require additional financial planning to fund that child's college. If we reexamine where our clients are in their lives, we can help them realign their strategy.

Once our clients have a clear plan, a few will feel they don't need to come in and meet with us anymore. We still encourage them to follow up periodically so that we maintain a close and helpful relationship. We keep in touch in a variety of ways, including a monthly newsletter we write ourselves. Most firms don't write their own newsletter, but we spend the time because we want to reinforce the core messages that we've taught our clients, and share what's going on in our firm. Regular communication helps keep the relationship strong, and ensures they keep moving toward their most important goals.

Some clients have deeply ingrained financial worries that never completely disappear, no matter how great their financial situation and plan are. They tend to want to come in every six months or so to review their circumstances with us, which is great. We can't change the way their brains are wired, but we can help significantly reduce their anxiety by reviewing the encouraging fundamentals of their assets and their strategy. Regardless of whether you lean toward going on autopilot or continuing to worry, working with a financial advisor can have a big emotional payoff.

Getting your financial house in order might feel complicated, confusing, overwhelming, and intimidating, particularly if you've also been managing the care of a child with mental illness. Maybe you're in your sixties now with an adult middle-aged child, and questions of wealth transfer and planning for after your death have been on the back burner until very recently. The good news is that you can still improve your situation. Developing and implementing an appropriate financial plan is doable, but you have to be proactive. The best time to start is today.

I encourage you to start taking steps now to plan for your own retirement, future needs, and long-term care as well as the needs of your dependent with mental illness. Even if you can't eliminate all of your challenges, every step you take will be significant. Even if you can only save a few hundred dollars here and there at first, that money will make a difference. An advisor can help you invest your savings as wisely as possible and stretch them as far as they'll go.

It's possible to go into a financial-planning office feeling overwhelmed and leave realizing that progress is possible. A professional advisor can partner with you and be in your corner to provide support as you tackle your challenges and pursue your goals. They can help you identify your most pressing problems as well as the appropriate solutions. They can offer empathy while maintaining a more neutral perspective to help you make good decisions. If you're feeling overwhelmed, you're not able to bring a clear head to problem-solving. A good advisor can help clarify the situation. That partnership can, in turn, alleviate your fear, anxiety, and worry so that you can get moving in the right direction.

# Acknowledgments

I want to thank my wife, Gayle, for her constant inspiration and for advocating not only for our son but also for everyone else's sons and daughters in Florida. She's become a major "NAG" for the NAMI Advocacy Group, raising essential awareness among legislators and showing them what needs to be done for the benefit of the mental health community. I want to thank my son, who, to this day, remains the bravest person I've ever met. I also want to thank my daughter for constantly challenging and delighting me.

There are whole armies of wonderful people working for and assisting mental health organizations like MHA and NAMI throughout the country. I have the utmost gratitude and respect for these people, but especially for my local NAMI chapter—NAMI-Broward—not only for all the help they've given my family directly in understanding mental illness, but also for all the work they do in Broward County and throughout the country. You guys are doing incredible work.

And for the families coping with severe mental illness, your continuing courage and resilience inspire me every day.

# About the Author

 **ALLEN GIESE** is the founder of Northstar Financial Planners, a fiduciary fee-only financial-planning firm in South Florida that prides itself on helping clients achieve what is most important to them. Allen is the father of an adult son who was diagnosed with schizophrenia in his late teens and, with his wife, Gayle, is deeply involved in mental health advocacy. Together, they founded Ride to Awareness; in 2015, Allen and his team rode three thousand miles, crossing the United States on bicycles to promote mental illness awareness and fighting the stigma attached to it. Both Allen and Gayle work closely with their local chapter of the National Alliance on Mental Illness. Allen speaks frequently on the unique challenges of special needs and mental health financial planning.